THE WORLD'S
GREATEST

SCANDALS
OF THE 20th CENTURY

THE WORLD'S GREATEST

SCANDALS

OF THE 20th CENTURY

EDITED BY

NIGEL BLUNDELL

PRINCIPAL CONTRIBUTORS:

GERRY BROWN
ROBIN CORRY
ALAN HALL

HAMLYN

To Carlos and Stan without whose support and succour this
book would not have been possible

First published in 1986 by Octopus Books Ltd

This edition published in 1994 by
The Hamlyn Publishing Group
an imprint of Reed Consumer Books Ltd
Michelin House, 81 Fulham Road
London SW3 6RB
and Auckland, Melbourne, Singapore and Toronto

ISBN 0 600 58610 3

A CIP catalogue record for this book is available from the
British Library

Printed in Great Britain by Cox & Wyman Ltd

Contents

Introduction

'Scandal is good, brisk talk,
whereas praise by one's
neighbour is by no means
lively hearing.
An acquaintance grilled, scored,
devilled and served with mustard
and cayenne pepper excites the
appetite, whereas a slice
of cold friend with currant
jelly is but a sickly,
unrelishing meal!'

William Makepeace Thackeray

Affairs of State

Edward Kennedy

Edward Moore Kennedy carried the hopes and dreams of millions of Americans who yearned for him to become the President of their country, the leader of the most powerful nation in the world and the man to whom they would happily entrust their destinies. They saw in him the same qualities with which they imbued his older brothers. The public viewed them as men of honesty and integrity, men who were brave, fearless and ferociously loyal to those close to them. It was a vision history was to question.

Both of Edward's brothers had died in the service of their country. The elder, President John Fitzgerald Kennedy, was slain by an assassin's bullet as he rode in a motorcade through the streets of Dallas, Texas, in November 1963, while five years later Robert Kennedy was struck down in a hail of gunfire in an hotel in Los Angeles, just as he had won an important campaign to become candidate for the Democratic Party to fight the 1968 presidential election.

After the murder of Robert Kennedy, the Democratic campaign to win control of the White House faltered and lost steam. The disheartened Democrats turned to former vice-president Hubert

Humphrey as their candidate. Humphrey was promptly defeated by Republican Richard Nixon, who scraped in with the lowest percentage of the popular vote for a winning President in more than five decades.

However, by 1969 it seemed that the fortunes of the Kennedy dynasty in American politics would be revived by Edward ('Teddy') Kennedy, then 37 years old and gaining rapidly in prestige and experience as a US Senator for his home state of Massachusetts.

American voters were increasingly attracted to Teddy Kennedy. He had the same ruggedly handsome looks as his brothers, and, apparently, the same strong-willed personality. With three years to go until another presidential contest, there was already a movement to groom the young Senator as a candidate for that election.

The prospect of candidacy for Teddy Kennedy vanished in a blaze of scandal in July 1969, when he left a young woman dead from drowning while he fled in selfish panic. For almost twelve hours the body of political secretary Mary Jo Kopechne was trapped in the rear seat of the Senator's car, which had plunged off a narrow bridge into an inlet of the Atlantic Ocean; and for twelve hours Teddy Kennedy's actions were those of a man frantically trying to set up an alibi for himself. Apparently desperate to keep the news of the car accident a secret, he failed to notify police or potential rescue services, hoping, he admitted later, that 'the sense of guilt would somehow be lifted from my shoulders'.

As Mary Jo Kopechne died choking for air in the rear seat of the flooded car, so too did the political ambitions of Teddy Kennedy and the faith the American public had in him.

Teddy Kennedy and his friends were familiar sights during the summer months in and around the fishing and yachting towns of Cape Cod and Nantucket Sound, where the Atlantic breakers pound at the shores of Massachusetts. For more than 30 years the Kennedy family had been taking part in the annual summer yachting regattas and races off the sandy beaches of the picturesque island of Martha's Vineyard.

There were cheers and friendly waves of recognition for Teddy Kennedy when he arrived at the harbour of Edgartown on Martha's Vineyard on the afternoon of 18 February 1969.

The starter's gun had fired an hour earlier to begin the first heat of the yacht races in the waters of the Nantucket Sound, and it looked as if Teddy Kennedy was determined to enjoy some sailing himself as he stripped off the jacket of his neat business suit and lounged back in his shirt sleeves on board the ferry for the three-minute ride from Martha's Vineyard to its neighbouring smaller island, Chappaquiddick.

Later that afternoon the Senator appeared even more relaxed, soaking up the sun at the helm of the blue-hulled yacht *Victura*, which he had inherited from his brother John, the late President. Looking fit and tanned, he cruised into Edgartown harbour and shared a celebration drink with the crew of the yacht *Bettawin*, who had triumphed in that first day's racing.

A short time later Kennedy joined the cheerful, milling crowd at the Shiretown Inn, overlooking the Edgartown Harbour, sipping a cool beer with a party of friends who included his cousin Joe Gargan and Kennedy family legal adviser Paul Markham. As evening fell the men strolled back down to the ferry landing, and once again they made the short trip back across the channel to Chappaquiddick Island.

By 8.30 that night they had joined three other men and six young women in a secluded rented cottage on Chappaquiddick, and as the flames from their barbecue lit up the night there was heady talk of top-level politics and the forthcoming battle for the presidency.

Among the guests was 29-year-old Mary Jo Kopechne, one of the enthusiastic 'boiler room' girls who had worked behind the scenes, for long hours with little reward other than gratitude, on the campaign to win the nomination for the late Senator Robert Kennedy in the presidential election of the previous year.

Mary Jo had been staying at the Dunes Hotel in Edgartown with her friend, law student Rosemary Keogh, 23. The two young women had arrived together at the Chappaquiddick cottage for the barbecue.

Three hours later Mary Jo left the cottage with Teddy Kennedy in his car. The car sped off towards the crossroads half a mile from the cottage, where a sharp left turn along the tarmac road would have taken them back to the ferry landing stage, facing the bright lights of Edgartown on the main island of Martha's Vineyard, just a hundred yards across the channel.

But the car turned right on to a rutted dirt road, away from the ferry and towards the thin strand of deserted beach on the eastern end of Chappaquiddick Island. The beach stretched out in a long peninsula, almost cut off from the island by a deep tidal 'lagoon' of the Atlantic Ocean. Across that inlet of water was the narrow wooden Dyke Bridge.

As the car sped on to the bridge, it skidded and plunged over the side into the chilly water. Unseen by any witnesses, it slipped beneath the waves. But a few seconds later, gasping for air, Senator Edward Kennedy bobbed to the surface and crawled to the safety of the beach.

Mary Jo Kopechne was still trapped inside.

Senator Kennedy explained later how he had mistaken the turning at the crossroads and how he had dived repeatedly into the surging waters, trying to rescue Mary Jo from the sunken car, after he had crashed from the bridge on the unfamiliar dirt road.

Exhausted by the effort, Kennedy rested for 15 minutes and then started running back towards the cottage where the barbecue was still in progress.

On his way back he passed a house only 200 yards from Dyke Bridge, but he never stopped to raise the alarm.

It was the Senator's behaviour when he finally reached the cottage which was to add even more fuel to the scandal.

Dripping wet Kennedy stayed outside in the garden and called for one of the partygoers to send Joe Gargan and Paul Markham out to talk to him.

In the darkness of the garden he explained what had happened and the two men bundled him into a car and drove immediately back to Dyke Bridge. Both Gargan and Markham stripped off and tried unsuccessfully to reach the trapped girl.

In despair all three men returned to their vehicle and drove off, leaving Mary Jo Kopechne behind, probably already dead — but just possibly trapped in an air pocket inside the sunken vehicle, struggling for her life. Again the men passed the house only a short distance from the bridge without making any attempt to raise the alarm.

At the inquest later Joe Gargan testified that Teddy Kennedy did not even want the other party guests at the cottage to be told of Mary Jo Kopechne's death.

James Mancham

Seychelles premier James Mancham's reputation as a ladies' man helped bring about his downfall. Mancham was ousted in a bloodless coup in 1977 at the age of 37. His country had gained independence from Britain only a year before and the premier was in London for the Commonwealth Prime Ministers' Conference when the news came through.

One of the glamourous girls that Mancham escorted said: 'Jimmy is admirable, handsome, charming and witty. He goes out with girls just as other heads of state do — but they keep their affairs under the stairs.'

Mancham made no attempt to keep his indulgences secret while he was in power. The whole world knew about his stunning girls, the expensive hotels, his love of 20-year-old claret. While still premier he said: 'In London I am a member of clubs like Annabelle's and Les Ambassadeurs. In New York I go to El Morocco. There are not so many third-world people in there. Back home they see it and say "Hey, what's that little bastard doing in there — he's one of us." It's power to the people!'

After the coup the new rulers accused him of 'adopting a lifestyle which involved lavish spending when the country and its people were working hard and making sacrifices to bring about prosperity and progress'.

Mancham settled down in London to live comfortably off his business interests.

The reaction of the man who aspired to be President of the United States was to break down in sobs of self-pity. He told his companions: 'This couldn't have happened, I don't know how it could have happened. Go back to the cottage but don't upset the other girls. Don't get them involved. I will take care of this.'

But Kennedy himself didn't want to return to the cottage. He asked the two men to drive him back to the crossroads and towards the Chappaquiddick ferry landing, the route he should have taken with Mary Jo when he left the barbecue.

At the ferry landing, Kennedy could have used a telephone to summon the ferryman from the other side to come and pick him up. But Gargan and Markham watched as he dived into the water and swam silently, with powerful strokes, across the channel to Edgartown.

Assuming he had gone to raise the alarm, the two men drove back to the cottage and rejoined the party. Gargan flopped down on a couch, explaining to one of the girls: 'Please let me lie down, I am exhausted.' But still neither of the men revealed anything of the drama which was still being played out.

In the darkness of Edgartown harbour, Teddy Kennedy slipped quietly out of the water and went straight to a room at the Shiretown Inn, which had been booked previously.

He changed into clean, dry clothes.

A few minutes later, calm and composed, Kennedy had yet another opportunity to alert the outside world to Mary Jo's fate.

Hotel owner Russ Peachey had been working late in his office. Several times that evening he had been interrupted by the sounds of revelry from rowdy parties of yachtsmen, and he had left his office to ask the merrymakers to be a little quieter. Now there was another disturbance, this time from the porch of the hotel annexe where Kennedy and his friends had their rooms.

Peachey peered out from his office and saw Kennedy fully dressed in a jacket and slacks. Kennedy had only just changed into the fresh clothes, yet when he saw Russ Peachey he explained to him: 'I have been asleep; something woke me up.'

Peachey sympathized: 'Must have been that loud party next door. I've already warned them about the noise.'

Kennedy seemed unperturbed. 'I seem to have misplaced my watch,' he told Peachey. 'Can you tell me what time it is?'

Peachey glanced over his shoulder to the clock on his office wall. 'It's twenty-five minutes after two. If you want to stay awake for a while I can let you have a portable TV set for your bedroom.'

Kennedy shrugged. 'No, thank you. Good night.' And he climbed back up the stairs to his bedroom.

In the hotel's small restaurant at 7.30 a.m. Kennedy sipped a cup of coffee. He looked none the worse for only five hours' sleep and he chatted to fellow yachtsmen about the prospects for that day's sailing competitions.

At 8.15 the first ferry of the day arrived from Chappaquiddick Island and two passengers, Joe Gargan and Paul Markham, hurried to meet Kennedy at his hotel.

By that time the upturned hulk of Kennedy's Oldsmobile limousine in the water beside Dyke Bridge had already attracted attention.

The ferry which had brought Gargan and Markham over to Martha's Vineyard had now taken Edgartown Police Chief Jim Arena over to Chappaquiddick Island.

Despite the influx of yachting visitors, it had been a quiet night for the Edgartown police department. A shopkeeper had reported a customer for leaving town without paying a bill, a lost wallet had been handed in and 18 cars had been given tickets for illegal parking.

The one call the chief decided to check out for himself had been telephoned to his office at 8.20 a.m.

Mrs Pierre Malm, the tenant of the house near Dyke Bridge, reported there was a car in the water.

Arena, a Massachusetts State Trooper for 13 years before he became Chief at Edgartown, had long regarded Dyke Bridge as a dangerous nuisance, with its low guard rails and the sharp bend halfway across its span. He assumed that a driver might have failed to position his car properly on the approach to the bridge, and had abandoned it stuck in the soft sand.

More irritating still to the meticulous police chief was the possibility that some irresponsible owner of a junk vehicle had simply dumped it off the bridge instead of paying for it to be taken to a scrapyard.

Only when he reached the bridge and saw the signs of the skid marks on its wooden surface did he begin to consider he might be facing a serious incident.

The tide was receding, and Arena could see it was a gleaming new vehicle and not a scrap car. Mrs Malm told him she had heard a car drive past her house at around midnight the night before, and Arena realized that there could be little hope for any occupant still inside the Oldsmobile who had not escaped at the time of the crash. Borrowing a face mask and swimming trunks, he tried to dive down to the car under six feet of water, but each time the rush of the ebbing tide swept him away.

On his radio Arena called for the help of John Farrar, the head of Edgartown's volunteer rescue department and a skilled sub-aqua diver. At the same time he asked his area headquarters to check the registration number of the vehicle — L78 207.

Back came the reply: 'It is registered to Senator Edward Kennedy.'

In his exhausting dives into the fast-flowing water, Arena had not been able to see if there was anyone still inside the car.

'My God,' he said to himself. 'Another tragedy for the Kennedys. That poor family.'

A few minutes later Farrar the diver plunged into the water with his oxygen tanks and began a thorough search. His first glimpse was hopeful. The driver's window was rolled completely down, allowing room for escape. The passenger window was still completely closed.

Only when Farrar inched round to the rear of the vehicle did he find Mary Jo's body.

Surfacing beside one of the piers of the bridge, he pulled the mask slowly from his face and called out quietly to Arena: 'There is someone in there. It is the body of a young blonde woman.'

He passed the police chief a brightly coloured handbag he had scooped from the rear of the car. Arena let the water trickle from the bag and then emptied out its contents: some cosmetics, a few dollar bills and a pass to the US Senate building.

He examined the pass. 'Well, at least we know now who she is,' he told Farrar. 'Her name is Rosemary Keogh, she must work for the Senator.'

At the same time Senator Edward Kennedy had arrived back on Chappaquiddick Island, accompanied by Gargan and Markham. But the three men made no attempt to go to the scene of Mary Jo's death. Instead they hung aimlessly around the ferry landing-stage.

By now the word was spreading of the grisly find at Dyke Bridge. Ferryman Dick Hewitt had heard the news, and he was puzzled why Kennedy and his companions should be making no move to visit Dyke Bridge and see for themselves. Seeing Kennedy at the landing stage, he called out to him, 'Senator, are you aware of this accident?'

One of Kennedy's friends replied: 'Yes, we've only just heard about it.'

Hewitt was even more puzzled when he cast off his ferry a few minutes later to return to Martha's Vineyard. Kennedy, Gargan and Markham were returning immediately with him to Edgartown.

Police Chief Arena was annoyed and frustrated when he discovered that Teddy Kennedy had been on Chappaquiddick Island less than an hour before and had not come to Dyke Bridge.

Arena borrowed a telephone and asked policewoman Carmen Salvador to check with Edgartown ferry stage to see if Kennedy was there. 'He is in your office now and he wants to speak to you,' she reported.

A few seconds later Teddy Kennedy, who had failed to report the accident nine hours earlier, spoke for the first time to a police official about the death of Mary Jo.

Arena was quick to offer sympathy.

'Senator, there has been an accident with your car and a girl is dead,' he told Kennedy.

Edward Kennedy returning to the US Senate after his car accident

'I know,' the Senator replied.

'Were there any other passengers in the car?' Arena asked fearfully. His heart sank when Kennedy replied: 'Yes, there were.'

Arena's mind was racing. 'Could they still be in the water?'

'No,' Kennedy replied with certainty. 'Can I see you in your office right away?'

Arena sped back to Edgartown. Meeting Kennedy for the first time in his office, he told him: 'I am sorry about the accident but I don't understand what has been happening.'

'It's all right, I know about it,' Kennedy admitted. 'I was the driver.'

Arena was stunned. 'Where does Rosemary Keogh come from? We must identify her next of kin.'

'It wasn't Rosemary,' Kennedy explained. 'It was Mary Jo Kopechne.'

Slowly Kennedy began to unfold his version of the horror of the previous night. He explained how he took the wrong turning at the crossroads, how his car had skidded on the bridge and of his futile attempts to rescue Mary Jo.

Arena listened in disbelief as Kennedy explained why he had not reported the accident. Kennedy told of his state of complete bewilderment and confusion after the crash, of his own injuries — concussion and abrasions of the scalp which had left him dazed.

Three days later, after he had rejoined his family, his three children and his wife Joan (who had just suffered a miscarriage), Teddy Kennedy was charged with leaving the scene of an accident and failing to report an accident. When he appeared in court his advocate Richard McCarron pleaded guilty on his behalf.

In spite of the blaze of publicity from the world's media, the case was tried just like any other motoring offence. The court was told by a probation officer that Kennedy had no previous convictions.

The decision of Judge James A. Boyle was a sentence of two months' imprisonment. The sentence was suspended.

For many diehard supporters of the young Prince of American politics, it was time to show their continuing blind loyalty to the Kennedy dynasty.

More than 30,000 telegrams of support flooded into his home in Hyannis Port. However, Teddy Kennedy's political ambitions had fallen from Dyke Bridge and shattered, and all the efforts of the political power brokers could never put them together again.

Rescue diver John Farrar was one of his bitterest critics. Farrar said after the court case: 'From receiving the call about the car to recovering Mary Jo's body took exactly 25 minutes. If I had been called that night there was no way she would have died. She had no fatal injuries, she died of drowning.

'She was alive a long time, at least one hour after the car went off the bridge. She must have been clawing and fighting for her life all that time. It was obvious she had reached up to a point in the car where there was still some air.

Nine hours afterwards there was still a bubble of air in the trunk of the car; it was barely damp.

'What Kennedy did was indefensible. He left that girl to die because he was only interested in saving his own skin.'

In the election of 1972, the Democratic choice to contest the White House against Richard Nixon was George McGovern.

Nixon won re-election.

Kennedy retained his seat in the US Congress as the Senator for Massachusetts. Ten years after the death of Mary Jo Kopechne, in 1979, there was a campaign to nominate Teddy Kennedy as the candidate to take over the Democratic Presidency from Jimmy Carter in the election contest against Ronald Reagan.

Before the campaign could get properly under way, the ghost of Mary Jo Kopechne was raised again, and Kennedy withdrew, apparently convinced that the power of the White House had been removed from his grasp for ever because of the scandal.

Before the 1972 election the name Chappaquiddick was known only to locals, tourists and yachtsmen as a sandspit of an island on the Atlantic Coast. Since then it has conjured up death, scandal and human frailty.

Only one other name of a featureless, mundane location can raise such a shock wave of political revulsion. Just like Chappaquiddick, it is burned indelibly into the history of scandal in American politics.

It is the name of a nondescript multi-storey office complex in Washington.

The block of cheap rental offices is called Watergate. . . .

The Profumo Affair

John Profumo was not the first cabinet minister to have an affair with a call-girl, but in unwittingly choosing one who was also the mistress of a Russian spy he sealed his own fate. His shamefaced confession and resignation on 5 June 1963 brought out into the open the most sensational sex scandal of the century.

As the facts of the case emerged, Profumo's humiliation and downfall were assured. But along with himself, he almost brought down the British government.

The key figure in this story of sex, duplicity and espionage was society osteopath Stephen Ward. He had what were described as 'healing hands', and it was this gift that allowed him to hobnob with the high and mighty.

Dr Ward, son of a clergyman, was vilified at his trial as 'a thoroughly filthy fellow' and 'a wicked, wicked creature'. But his motives were, by modern standards, far from unusual. He liked to cultivate friends in high places, many of whom he first met as patients. And he loved the company of beautiful women.

As an ordinary medical man, he could not hope to compete for the society ladies, so he would seek out beautiful girls from humble backgrounds, install them at his flat and groom them for greater things.

Many of his 'discoveries' were working in nightclubs when they first met Ward. Often, introduced to his society friends, they took the opportunity to become high-class prostitutes.

One such girl was beautiful brunette Christine Keeler. Christine was just 16 when she came to London to work in a nightclub — a job which involved no more than, to use her own words, 'walking around with no clothes on'. At the club she met Ward, who developed a Svengali-like hold over her. He took her home to his flat, introduced her to drugs and orgies and persuaded her to sleep with his influential clients.

As an osteopath, Ward numbered among his clients many wealthy, influential and titled people. As an accomplished artist, he had drawn many of them. Chattering to clients during their treatment, Ward had expressed the wish to go to Moscow to draw some of the Russian leaders, particularly Khrushchev, but he was having difficulty getting a visa.

One client, *Daily Telegraph* editor Sir Colin Coote, who was being treated for lumbago, introduced him to an assistant Russian naval attaché, Captain Eugene Ivanov, whom Coote had met during a visit to the newspaper by Soviet officials. Ward and Ivanov, a hard-drinking ladies' man who spoke excellent English, soon became firm friends.

Another of Ward's clients was Lord Astor, one of the richest men in England, who got to know the osteopath when he went to him for treatment after a hunting accident. Astor allowed Ward to use a cottage on his estate at Cliveden, and it was here that the scheming medical man would invite his friends for boisterous weekends.

Two of the guests on such a visit were Ivanov and Keeler. They became lovers.

On another occasion when Keeler visited Cliveden, a second remarkable meeting occurred . . . between Christine Keeler the prostitute and John Profumo the cabinet minister.

Lord Astor allowed Ward and his guests to use the estate's private swimming pool. Christine Keeler was bathing there in the nude one day when she heard voices and saw the peer, his wife and another man and woman approaching. She squealed for her swimsuit, but Ward grabbed it and tossed it out of reach.

She scrambled out of the pool and grabbed a towel to cover her blushes — but not before the peer and his companions had enjoyed her embarrassment.

The man with Lord Astor liked what he saw and was determined to see even more. He was John Profumo, war minister in the Conservative government. With him on the visit to Cliveden was his wife, actress Valerie Hobson.

After returning home from the Cliveden weekend, Profumo got in touch with Keeler through Ward. He borrowed a ministerial car and took her for a drive to see the Houses of Parliament and the prime minister's Downing Street residence. He gave her gifts and money and the cabaret girl and the cabinet minister became lovers. He often met her for sex sessions at Ward's flat. So did Ivanov. As one lover left the other would arrive, and the two men narrowly missed each other on several occasions.

It was at this stage that Britain's MI5, the counter-espionage agency, became seriously disturbed. Because of his contacts with leading politicians, Ward had already been checked out by MI5 and passed as 'clean'. But according to more than one expert who has researched the case since, the security men had been making good use of Ward's contacts.

MI5 were said to have used Ward when they wanted pretty but discreet female company for visiting diplomats. They had turned to him again when they wanted information about Ivanov, whom they knew to be a spy.

But when Profumo came on the scene, MI5 became anxious. They suggested that Sir Norman Brook, then secretary of the Cabinet, have words with the minister. Sir Norman tried to make it clear to Profumo that he had blundered into a delicate security operation, but Profumo thought he was simply being warned to steer away from Ward and his loose ladies, and he was far too infatuated with his inventive mistress to take the matter seriously.

Ivanov, meanwhile, knew perfectly well that MI5 were trying to trap him, and he reported every detail back to Moscow. He also discovered that Ward had a collection of pornographic photographs, some showing politicians and diplomats in bed with girls. Ivanov sent copies back to his Russian masters — presumably for blackmail purposes.

Profumo eventually ended the affair with Keeler, writing her a farewell letter that began 'Darling . . .' Any scandal, he no doubt thought, had been prevented.

The case could have ended there, except for a bizarre twist that was to seal the fate of all those involved. . . .

Stephen Ward wanted to go to bed with a coloured girl, and asked Christine Keeler to procure one for him. He took her to a café where West Indians were smoking marijuana, and after buying some drugs she allowed herself to be picked up by one of the customers, 'Lucky' Gordon. There was one proviso, however: before she would go off with her new boyfriend, he must provide a black girl for her 'brother', Ward.

The affair between Ward and the girl developed until she left him, first for Keeler's boyfriend Gordon and later for another coloured man, John Edgecombe. Keeler herself, having left Ward for Gordon, finally left Gordon for Edgecombe.

These extraordinarily tangled love affairs created intense jealousies. When Christine arrived at a nightclub with Edgecombe, Gordon appeared on the scene, a fight developed and the latter had to have 17 stitches in a face wound. Edgecombe went on the run with Keeler but she tired of him and returned to the relative harmony of Ward's home, where he was now living with another girl — Marilyn Rice-Davies, better known as Mandy.

Edgecombe tracked her down, and when she would not open the door he fired shots at the lock and at the window. He was arrested and charged . . . and the first cracks in the secrecy surrounding the scandal began to appear.

By the time the case came up, Christine, one of the principal witnesses, had disappeared. Instead of giving evidence in court, she was dining out on her amazing story with anyone who would listen. At a Christmas party two of the guests took her seemingly fanciful tales seriously. One was a friend of prominent Labour politician George Wigg and the other was acquainted with a Sunday newspaper reporter. Throughout the corridors of power and up and down Fleet Street, the rumours began to spread.

Christine sold the story to the *Sunday Pictorial*. It was written but never published. Word got back to Profumo. With a brazenness which was astonishing, he immediately sought appointments with the Attorney General and senior Conservative party officials. He told them that any suggestion of an affair with Christine was untrue and that if the allegation was published in a newspaper he would sue for libel.

On 21 March 1963 George Wigg rose to his feet in the House of Commons and with parliamentary privilege told the world about the rumours concerning the cabinet minister and the call-girl.

Profumo immediately drafted a statement which he later read to the house. He denied that he had had an affair with Christine Keeler, and concluded: 'I shall not hesitate to issue writs for libel and slander if scandalous allegations are made or repeated outside this house.'

Christine backed up his denial with a newspaper interview in which she said: 'It was a friendship no one can criticize'.

Profumo went on to repeat the lies directly to Prime Minister Harold Macmillan. The urbane Macmillan, a man who believed implicitly in the gentleman's code of conduct, accepted the word of his minister.

But the rumours persisted, particularly on the Continent, and Profumo had to sue one Italian magazine. The police received anonymous phone calls accusing Ward of living off immoral earnings, and alleging that he was being protected by friends in high places. They talked to Keeler, who gave them a statement admitting that she had slept with Profumo, and even describing in detail his bedroom.

Ward knew that the police were making inquiries, and started writing letters to influential people in the hope of staing off prosecution. One of the letters was foolishly sent to the opposition leader, Harold Wilson. As the scandal grew, the prime minister at last ordered the Lord Chancellor to launch an inquiry.

Now guilt was beginning to plague Profumo. He confided in his wife, and they decided that he must tell the truth. They broke short a holiday and returned to Britain. He saw the Prime Minister's private secretary and said: 'I have to tell you that I did sleep with Miss Keeler and my statement in that respect was untrue.'

He immediately resigned. Such was his shame that he declined to follow the tradition of handing his seals of office personally to the Queen, and instead sent a messenger to Buckingham Palace.

Shortly afterwards ill-health forced Macmillan to resign. The Conservatives were heavily defeated at the next general election, with many members of the party blaming the Profumo affair.

The tragedy did not end with the belated confession of John Profumo. Stephen Ward was brought to court charged with living off the immoral earnings of Keeler and Mandy Rice-Davies. The judge started to sum up in the case, but did not have time to finish that day. When the court resumed the following morning it was learned that Ward had taken a drugs overdose. He was found guilty in his absence and the judge postponed sentence until he was well enough to appear again in the dock.

But Ward never regained consciousness. He died on 3 August 1963.

An exhaustive inquiry into the Profumo affair was ordered under the redoubtable judge Lord Denning, but it was not until many years later that Stephen Ward's links with MI5 were investigated. They were outlined by David Lewis in his book *Sexpionage* and by Nigel West in his book *A Matter Of Trust (MI5 1945–72)*.

West's book prompted the *Sunday Times* to make its own inquiries. It asked a retired senior MI5 officer if the court could not have been told that Ward was working for the security service. He replied: 'Yes, Ward might be alive today if that had happened. We didn't expect the final outcome, and we were very cut up when we learned he was dead.'

The other members of the cast of this extraordinary melodrama played out on a world stage fared variously.

Eugene Ivanov slipped quietly back to Moscow for praise and promotion.

Mandy Rice-Davies also left the country, singing on the continental cabaret circuit at the age of 19 before marrying an Israeli airline steward she met in a Tel Aviv night-club. They built up a chain of restaurants and clubs before divorcing, at which time Mandy returned to Britain to find relative happiness and success as an actress.

But for Christine Keeler, the death of Ward signalled the end of the high life. She had been bewitched by the bright lights and big names, bemused and flattered by the attentions and gifts that rich, important men lavished on a pretty teenager.

Lord Denning, in his inquiry into the affair, said: 'Let no one judge her too harshly. She was not yet 21. And since the age of 16 she had become enmeshed in a web of wickedness.'

In the years after the Profumo scandal she had two disastrous marriages, spent a few months in jail, faced a legal battle for custody of her child and ended up virtually penniless in a West London council flat.

And John Profumo? Once the dust had settled, he began working unpaid at Toynbee Hall, an organization in London's East End that helps the poor, the mentally handicapped, alcoholics — anyone with a social problem. In the years following the scandal, he was awarded the CBE, had friendly chats with the Queen, was appointed to the board of a leading insurance company founded by his grandfather, joined the board of visitors of a psychiatric prison at the invitation of the then home secretary James Callaghan and was considered for a peerage.

Mandy Rice-Davies at her Kensington home

The Prince of Wales and Mrs Langtry

Lillie Langtry was the most outrageous 'scarlet woman' of her time. Monarchs and millionaires, princes and playwrights queued to win her affection — or just to admire the smouldering beauty that made her the talk of London and Parisian society. She was passionate, sensuous, spellbindingly beautiful . . . and she didn't give a damn. Lillie Langtry was made for scandal — and when that scandal broke, it was not over some obscure Lord. It was with the future King of England.

The affair — at a time when such indiscretions were kept 'under wraps' — turned her into the most celebrated 'other woman' in the land, and the Prince of Wales into the happiest man. Both threw decorum to the wind for a passionate, tempestuous romance.

Lillie was born in Jersey as Emilie Charlotte Le Breton, a clergyman's daughter, in 1854. She had six brothers, and spent her childhood days as a tomboy — far removed from the ambitious beauty she was to become. One theory is that she inherited her passions from her father — the 'Dirty Dean', as he was known for his unholy behaviour with many of the island's young ladies.

It wasn't long before the eligible bachelors were soon pursuing her on the island, though her father had to warn her away from her first suitor, because he was one of the philandering dean's illegitimate children. Undaunted, she continued her little flings on Jersey with a steady stream of admirers.

But level-headed Lillie was determined to rise above the social stratum into which she was born. A brief trip to London and its glittering social scene, where the women wore crinoline dresses as wide as their height, and French hats adorned their rolling curls, was enough to convince her that marriage was for advancement and not for love.

When she did marry morose widower Edward Langtry in March 1874 it was because he was wealthy — and she admired his yacht. Quite unashamedly in later years, she was to say: 'To become the mistress of the yacht, I married the owner.' The marriage took them to Hampshire, then on to London, where Lillie insisted on living so she could recuperate after a fierce bout of typhoid fever.

It was her wish to be in London society permanently, and in 1875 it came true. She entered a world of exquisite good taste and wealth. She dined at the homes of the famous and captivated every male guest.

It was at one such party that the famous portrait artist George Francis Miles sketched her. Later, the vision of loveliness with the noble face and inviting red lips was reproduced on cards for a penny a time. The portraits were to go into thousands of humble homes — and the regal abode of His Royal Highness the Prince of Wales. When he saw her face, he was hopelessly hooked. It was then a mere formality for Edward — 'Bertie' to his friends — to get to meet her.

A friend in league with the 36-year-old heir to the throne arranged a dinner party at which the prince was the surprise guest. Lillie was to confess later in life that she thought then the whole scenario had been rigged . . . so that Bertie could get a glimpse of the woman all London was talking about. He was not displeased with what he saw. As her husband stood, frantically bowing at her side, he had already made up his mind that this was a woman he would see more of.

Neither were novices to the illicit game about to be played out. Bertie had wooed and won more than a dozen women. The affairs were always discreet, always controlled and always kept out of the papers. Lillie had cavorted with the wealthy, the social élite of London, the King of the Belgians — even, it was rumoured, Oscar Wilde.

This was to be different. Bertie flaunted the most glamorous woman of the age like a proud schoolboy showing off his first sweetheart. He built a house for her at fashionable Bournemouth, which was to be the hideaway for their lovemaking weekends. He took her to Paris, where he stayed at the elegant Hotel Bristol — and didn't care who saw her. It was even rumoured that once he kissed her in full view of everybody at Maxim's restaurant. By 1878 Britain was buzzing with gossip that Lillie Langtry was his mistress.

Still the affair continued, and still with the veneer of respectability. At functions such as Cowes or Ascot, both lovers would attend. But Lillie would always be escorted by her husband, and the Prince by his wife Alexandra.

It seems inconceivable that Princess Alexandra should not have known of her husband's infidelity, when all Society was talking about it. Anti-royalist pamphlets lampooned the Prince and Mrs Langtry. Yet even in the outwardly strict and moralist Victorian era, somehow the relationship survived . . . until both she and Edward were captivated by new lovers.

After three torrid years, the Prince became infatuated with Sarah Bernhardt, the Parisian actress of the Comédie Française. Lillie became the companion of Prince Louis of Battenberg, the dashing naval officer regarded as one of the best-looking men in Britain at that time. It was as if the insatiable wanderlust in both Bertie and his darling Lillie had driven them apart.

Even though they were now no longer sharing the same bed, the Prince of Wales — later to become King Edward VII — always remained on good terms with Lillie. She became pregnant by Prince Louis, father of the late Earl Mountbatten, and had an illegitimate

The Prince of Wales

Mrs Langtry

daughter. The Prince remained in constant touch when she went to France to give birth to Jeanne Marie, although Louis was never to be her lover again — devoting himself instead to a naval career which he would not jeopardize for a scandalous relationship.

Lillie went from strength to strength. She became an actress, travelled America, and even had the town of Vinegaroon in Texas renamed Langtry in her honour. There followed more affairs after the death of her husband Edward in 1897 until she was remarried, to baronet's son Hugo de Bathe, and became in due course Lady de Bathe.

In an age of hypocrisy, when women were treated as the underdogs, Lillie Langtry (who lived until 1929) had turned the tables and made her charm, beauty and sex appeal work for her.

The 'Jersey Lily' is now buried in a quiet churchyard on her native island . . . near the grave of one of her first loves.

John Vassall

The top-priority telephone call from the headquarters of the Central Intelligence Agency in Langley, Virginia, to the British Embassy 20 miles away in Washington DC was an urgent warning, calling for drastic action. The CIA had discovered that the most sensitive military secrets of the Royal Navy's role in the North Atlantic Treaty Organization were being betrayed by a spy inside the heart of the Admiralty building in Whitehall.

Although incalculable damage had already been done, the CIA were confident that the traitor would be unmasked and his flow of information to his Soviet spymaster halted within a matter of days. But London's reaction to the vital tip-off was to provoke a reaction which sent Anglo-US intelligence relations to an all-time low and led to one of the most damaging spy scandals ever to blacken the reputation of the spy-catchers of MI5.

MI5 were smugly convinced that the Americans were being duped into sending them on a wild-goose chase, an elaborate hoax by a defector to spread alarm in the West and to tie up counter-espionage services on a time-wasting exercise which would only throw false suspicion on blameless, loyal civil servants.

It wasn't until March 1962, three months after the defection of KGB agent Anatoli Golytsin, that MI5 officers travelled to the United States to interview him. And despite the fact that the defector, who had sought asylum for himself and his family, had already identified a widespread spy network in France and uncovered a Canadian ambassador as a traitor, the British remained sceptical.

The MI5 officers explained patiently that their thorough method of positive vetting — scrutinizing in great detail the background of everyone with access to secrets — made it virtually impossible for the Soviets to plant a traitor in a position of responsibility. Bowing to pressure from the Americans, they did eventually agree to begin a discreet hunt for the unknown spy, but in the face of the growing frustration of the Americans, the investigation went on for a further five months without result.

Then, to the embarrassment of MI5, the persistent CIA men who gave them the first hint of the existence of the spy turned up trumps again with the exact details of the traitor's identity. Another of their sources, a Soviet official based at the United Nations, had provided the last clue in the jigsaw. The traitor was a homosexual official who had been blackmailed while serving on the diplomatic staff of the British Embassy in Moscow.

This could fit only one man, William John Christopher Vassall, then 38 years old, a clerk in the Fleet Section of Military Branch II and a former assistant private secretary to the Civil Lord of the Admiralty. Vassall had served as clerk to the naval attaché in Moscow between 1954 and 1956 after training in the Royal Air Force as a photographer. Since he had taken up his job at the Admiralty, hundreds of secret documents had passed over his desk.

The first task of the spy-catchers was to borrow a neighbour's home next door to Vassall's bachelor flat in Dolphin Square, on the Thames Embankment in Chelsea, to keep watch on him. Knowing he was safely at his office, MI5 'burglars' expertly let themselves into his flat — and their worst fears were confirmed.

Inside they found his miniature Exacta camera with rolls of film of Admiralty documents, all hidden inside a specially constructed book-case. On 12 September 1962 Vassall was arrested as he left the Admiralty building, and was charged with espionage. At interrogation sessions with Special Branch detectives, he willingly poured out his tale of personal misery and anguish. A lonely introvert, Vassall the junior clerk had felt overwhelmed and ill at ease with the social life of his Embassy colleagues and had struck up a friendship with a young Russian civilian employed at the Embassy as an interpreter and liaison clerk. The handsome young Russian, Mikhailski, was a KGB agent who enticed the vulnerable Vassall into a homosexual affair.

Vassall took comfort in his association with the Russian and their frequent visits to the theatre, ballet and restaurants — until he was rebuked by a superior for his socializing.

A few months later the KGB experts in sexual compromise made their major effort, luring Vassall to a party at the Hotel Berlin, where

John Vassall

he was plied with drink until almost senseless and persuaded to take part in a homosexual orgy. Bitterly ashamed, he could not bring himself to confess to his seniors at the Embassy.

He decided to live with his guilty secret. Homosexual practices were still an offence in Britain and a serious crime under Soviet law.

The KGB trap was sprung before he was reassigned to duties in London. He was invited to a private apartment in Moscow, where a senior KGB official produced photographs of the orgy.

Vassall was told by the Russians that he would be able to leave the Soviet Union without being arrested and facing a possible jail term . . . but only if he agreed to continue a series of meetings in London with a KGB agent who was at the Moscow blackmail showdown.

Vassall returned to England and his new job at the Admiralty. Under the threat of exposure of his homosexuality, he began to pass secrets to the Russian agent Gregory at meetings at London underground stations and in telephone boxes.

The betrayal of secrets continued until the CIA cracked the case. In 1962 Vassall was convicted of espionage and sentenced to 18 years in jail. He was paroled after 10.

Under public pressure the government set up an inquiry under Lord Radcliffe to examine the background to the Vassall case. The complacent MI5 experts were forced to admit that their supposedly infallible positive vetting methods had failed miserably.

John Vassall would have been an obvious security risk even to a casual observer. Two of the 'referees' he gave to vouch for his character were elderly ladies, one of whom even warned her Security Service interviewer that Vassall 'took very little interest in the opposite sex'. In spite of all the danger signs, he was cleared for access to top secrets.

The tribunal did little to ease public outrage over the scandal. However, it did take action against two Fleet Street journalists who wrote in their reports of the Admiralty spy that many of his colleagues knew he was a homosexual. Able to keep a secret better than MI5, the journalists refused to reveal the sources of their information and were sentenced to prison terms.

King Carol

King Carol of Romania lost his throne in 1925 because of his flagrant affair with his mistress, Magda Lupescu. Five years later he was back — displacing his own son and installing Magda in an ornate mansion near his palace. King Carol finally got his marching orders in 1940, when Romania's pro-Nazi government kicked him and his mistress out of the country. They left their homeland on a September night, lying together on the floor of a train as bullets from angry demonstrators whistled above their heads.

Lord Lambton

The sneak photographs were lurid and titillating. They showed quite clearly a middle-aged man relaxing on a bed with two prostitutes unaware of the camera, and puffing contentedly on a hand-rolled cigarette.

They might have served as useful ammunition for a blackmailer wanting to embarrass the unsuspecting customer who had been visiting the prostitutes at the elegant second-floor flat in an expensive apartment block in Maida Vale, London.

But 'the purpose of the photographs — taken by a cameraman hidden inside a wardrobe, and concealed by a two-way mirror — wasn't to put pressure on the client for money or favours to cover up his sexual indiscretions.

The object was instead to expose him in public in exchange for a fat fee from a newspaper publisher.

For the man in the photographs was not some unwise, adulterous businessman with a modest reputation and suburban family life at stake.

He was Lord Lambton, a cabinet minister serving in the sensitive post of parliamentary under-secretary at the Ministry of Defence, a senior politician in charge of the Royal Air Force.

And despite the fact that 51-year-old Anthony Lambton would be facing the certain end of his political career and a public scandal which could destroy his personal life, there was never the slightest possibility that he would submit to blackmail to preserve his guilty secret.

The man who held the key to the fate of Lord Lambton was 28-year-old Colin Levy, an unemployed taxi driver with a petty criminal record and a habit of heavy drinking which left him always short of money. Early in 1973, Levy's only source of income was the earnings of his beautiful wife Norma, 26, a prostitute who made her living by indulging the sexual whims of wealthy clients.

For two years, since shortly after their marriage, Norma had worked as a call-girl for an escort agency, while her husband had driven her to a series of clandestine meetings with her clients in expensive hotels in London's West End. Colin Levy rarely, if ever, met the men who handed over large sums of money to his wife.

But the situation changed when the couple managed to acquire enough money to rent their own apartment in Maida Vale, in one of London's more expensive inner suburbs. Then Norma was able to 'work from home', leaving Colin Levy more time to indulge his own fantasies of striking it rich, while he frittered away his wife's immoral earnings in pubs and expensive drinking clubs.

Occasionally by chance, Levy would brush shoulders with his wife's customers as they came and went at the apartment, and it was only a matter of time before the scheming taxi driver began to wonder if any of them could be worth even more than the exorbitant fees they paid to his wife for her sexual services.

One regular customer in particular caught his attention; the tall, aristocratic 'Mr Lucas', whose frequent visits to the apartment would include sex sessions with Norma and a black girl, Kim, and smoking cigarettes heavily laced with cannabis.

But 'Mr Lucas' looked destined to remain just another anonymous contributor to the Levys' modest income, no different from any of the other furtive clients who used an alias to book appointments discreetly by telephone.

It was only after a number of visits to the Maida Vale apartment that 'Mr Lucas' began to drop hints that he was an important political figure. Norma Levy, who realized that the ability to keep bedroom secrets was essential to maintain a confidential relationship with her regular customers, was unimpressed. She had heard that kind of boastful talk before.

Whoever 'Mr Lucas' really was, his face was unfamiliar. He was certainly not a celebrity who would be readily recognized in the street. But Colin Levy was intrigued.

The mystery client quite openly gave away his true identity after one visit to Norma Levy when he rummaged through his wallet and found he was short of cash. From his jacket pocket he pulled out his cheque book and scribbled out a £50 payment.

Casually he wrote his name.

Anthony Claud Frederick Lambton, the sixth Earl of Durham, one of the wealthiest men in Britain, had just signed his own political and social death warrant.

Almost immediately Colin Levy began to lay a trap. He knew it would be an act of criminal blackmail to make any demands for large sums of money from Lord Lambton himself, but he also realized that if there was no cash to be gained in committing a crime and covering up a potential scandal, there could be a small fortune to be made, quite legally, by openly revealing the whole affair.

Lord Lambton would not be made to pay for his indiscretions, Levy decided. On the other hand, scandal-hungry newspaper and magazine publishers might.

But a cheque signed by Lord Lambton and the testimony of the taxi driver and his prostitute wife were obviously not going to be enough to convince any editor wary of the pitfalls of England's notoriously punishing libel laws. Levy needed irrefutable, independent evidence of the identity of his wife's most celebrated customer.

It took him only a couple of days and an outlay of a few pounds to

Lord Lambton, at home, shortly after his resignation from the Government

install a new piece of furniture in the bedroom of the Maida Vale apartment — a spacious wardrobe with a two-way mirror taking up most of its door frame.

The next visit of 'Mr Lucas' was meticulously chronicled by Levy, with a camera behind the two-way mirror silently capturing the scene on a roll of colour film. Hidden inside a giant toy teddy bear, propped innocently on a chair in a corner, was a tape recorder registering every word of the conversation, including the trusting client's admission that he had often smoked cannabis-drugged cigarettes.

Here was the proof Colin Levy was looking for. He gathered his evidence and approached Fleet Street's most popular newspaper with his sensational scoop.

Levy expected to be met with disbelief from cynical executives of the newspaper when he unfolded his scandalous allegations. They listened carefully to the details of Lord Lambton's sexual escapades.

But the shocking story of the Royal Air Force minister's visits to prostitutes was no secret to the journalists of the *News of the World*. For months they had been conducting their own investigation into whispers of a ring of prostitutes who catered for important politicians and government officials, and much of what Colin Levy had to say was not new to them.

Levy left Fleet Street with an arrangement for a qualified photographer to take photographs of Lord Lambton's next visit to Maida Vale. Armed with the new set of photographs, he had another meeting in the offices of the newspaper, and he named his price for exposing Lord Lambton to scandal, ridicule and disgrace — £30,000.

But the newspaper's own dossier on Lord Lambton was virtually complete. Levy, with his folder of compromising photographs, tape recordings and the uncashed cheque, was firmly shown the door. They didn't want to do business with him. With visions of his potential windfall rapidly vanishing, he panicked and began trying to peddle his story to other Fleet Street newspapers, and to the correspondents of overseas magazines.

The journalists for the mass circulation German magazine *Stern* leafed through Colin Levy's bulky file on Lord Lambton with open enthusiasm. They carefully interviewed him about the background to the entire scandal and they listened patiently to his insistence that he would not part with his corroborating photographs and tapes without a massive payment of cash. They declined to pay him a penny.

But unhindered by English libel law, the German magazine decided they had enough material to publish a sensational exposé of tales of high-ranking politicians, diplomats, brothels and prostitutes.

As news of the impending *Stern* article leaked to Fleet Street, the *News of the World* decided they should inform Scotland Yard of their own investigations. The newspaper's editorial team had been examining not only Lord Lambton, but at least one other unnamed senior politician.

On 21 May, 1973, as Colin and Norma Levy fled from England to Spain, unrewarded for their efforts in trying to sell the secret of Lord Lambton's shame, the peer was ushered into a fifth-floor office at New Scotland Yard. He had arrived there at the invitation of two of the Yard's most senior men, Deputy Assistant Commissioner Ernie Bond and top investigator Commander Bert Wickstead.

Lambton paced up and down the room, refusing the polite offer of a seat, his coat draped from his shoulders like a cape. He glared at the two policemen when they confronted him with the statements and photographs from the files of the Fleet Street newspapermen.

With an air of disdain, he admitted he knew Norma Levy.

'Yes, I've been to bed with her,' he confessed casually. 'She's a kind of prostitute.'

The policemen listened in silence. They knew that Lord Lambton had just thrown away his political career.

However, a sexual transaction between a prostitute and her client is no crime, and Deputy Assistant Commissioner Bond immediately turned to the subject which warranted a top-level police investigation of the Peer's private life.

'Have you taken drugs in her presence?' he asked.

Suddenly the air of aristocratic arrogance vanished. Lord Lambton stopped pacing the room and slumped in a chair.

In a voice muted with shame he admitted that he had first smoked cannabis twenty years earlier while visiting China, and he confirmed that the cigarette he was smoking in the photographs with Norma Levy and the black girl, Kim, was probably drugged.

Bond and Wickstead watched as the peer rose slowly to his feet and began to strip off his clothes, down to his red flannel underwear, anxious to prove to the policemen that he had no needle marks from injections of powerful narcotics.

Two hours later, both detectives watched as Lord Lambton knelt down beside the skirting board in the study of his home in St John's Wood, a short distance from Norma Levy's apartment. From inside a concealed cupboard he produced a small plastic box containing cannabis and amphetamine tablets.

'I confiscated them from a friend,' he tried to explain, 'and I hid them there to prevent my wife or children finding them.'

Now he faced not only political disgrace but a criminal prosecution for possession of drugs.

As he left the house to be escorted back to Scotland Yard the full realization of his predicament almost overwhelmed him.

'This is the end of my political career,' he said quietly. 'I shall resign as soon as I return to my office.'

The headlines which Colin Levy had wrongly imagined would make him rich were blazoned all over the world's press next day.

In a statement of shame mixed with anger, Lord Lambton declared publicly:

This is the sordid story. There has been no security risk and no blackmail and never at any time have I spoken of any aspect of my late job. All that has happened is that some sneak pimp has seen an opportunity of making money by the sale of the story and secret photographs to papers at home and abroad.

My own feelings may be imagined but I have no excuses whatsoever to make. I behaved with credulous stupidity.

Ironically the words of Lord Lambton from ten years earlier had come back to haunt him. . . .

Jerry Brown

California Governor Jerry Brown's long-standing relationship with sexy rock star Linda Rondstadt scandalized political circles. At one time Brown proposed to Linda, who is reported to have accepted. But after speculation that the marriage could wreck both their careers, word came out that the nuptials were off. The friendship continued, however.

Linda once posed for a promotional poster dressed only in hotpants and roller skates. At a New Jersey concert she swayed so enthusiastically that she popped out of her scoop-necked blouse, to the delight of her audience and her boyfriend's political enemies.

Other vote-losers were reckoned to have been her reported comments on sex and drugs. She once said: 'I love sex as much as I love music. And I think it's as hard to do.'

Linda often accompanied Brown to official functions. She horrified staid Washington matrons by wearing jeans to a reception given by Nancy Kissinger. At another, wearing a dress, she waited until photographers were ready to snap her and Brown, then hitched her skirt to give them a flash of thigh.

In 1963, Lambton, the Member of Parliament for the Conservative rural constituency of Berwick-on-Tweed, the heart of his family's massive land holdings, had been one of the first politicians to hear the rumours of an affair between war minister John Profumo and call-girl Christine Keeler.

In an article in one of the newspapers now filled with the story of his own disgrace, Lambton had written pompously: 'I warned the Conservative Party but no one took any notice. One cannot help regretting the whole of this squalid affair. It is the beginning of another unfortunate chapter which may end heaven knows where.'

But for many of his political foes, and even a few of his friends, Lambton's downfall seemed like the fulfilment of the prophecies of doom and disaster which surrounded his family.

The Lambton family had owned much of the sprawling northern area of County Durham since the days of the Norman Conquest, but not without a price. According to medieval legend the deadly personal ill-fortune of the Lambtons began with the return of John de Lambton after a gruelling crusade in the Holy Land.

At the gates of Lambton Castle, the tired and dishevelled knight was confronted with a monster barring his way. He drew his heavy crusader's sword and slashed it through the neck. With its dying breath the monster is recorded in folklore to have warned John de Lambton he would have to kill the next creature he saw or 'nine generations of your family will carry a curse'.

Legend has it that moments later the crusader's father, Robert de Lambton, ran from the castle gates to greet his son. Even though fearful of the curse, John de Lambton could not bring himself to kill his own father. So the curse, and the legend, stuck.

Lord Lambton had not expected to inherit the title. The honour only came to him in 1940 when he was a shy and sickly teenager. His elder brother John, then 20, died a painful death in a shooting accident in the grounds of Lambton Park, surrounding the family's stately home.

The new heir to the title struggled to fill the place of his brother, an athletic all-round sportsman.

Young Anthony immediately joined the Army, and after reaching the rank of corporal he was packed off to join the sons of other noble aristocrats for officer training at Sandhurst. He was invalided out, though, because of asthma and poor eyesight and spent the rest of the war as a fitter at a Tyneside shipyard, working on the factory floor alongside many men whose families were humble tenants of the lordly Lambton estates.

On a training trip to a workshop in London, he met another unlikely factory hand, 19-year-old Belinda Blew-Jones, daughter of a retired Army officer. The pair were promptly married. Their daughter Lucinda was born the following year, and over the next 15 years they had four other daughters.

Lambton was only 22 years old when he fought, and lost, his first parliamentary election in County Durham in 1945, when peacetime voters swung solidly towards a Labour government.

Six years later, using all the influence of his aristocratic title, and the persuasive powers of his father, the fifth Earl of Durham, he was given the Conservative nomination to 'inherit' the electorally safe Conservative seat of Berwick-on-Tweed, where his family owned many of their estates. On his election, he quickly gained a succession of junior appointments in the government.

When in 1961 his son Edward was born, in outdated baronial style he ordered fireworks and the roasting of an ox in Lambton Park as a public celebration.

In 1970, when Britain was poised for another general election, Anthony Lambton had a stark choice. His father had died and the title of Earl of Durham had passed to Anthony, yet to accept it would have barred him from standing for election to the Commons.

Faced with the option of a largely ceremonial seat in the House of Lords or the prospect of real power in the Commons, he chose to renounce the earldom. A grateful Edward Heath rewarded him with the important appointment of Minister for the Royal Air Force.

Two years later a privileges committee in the Commons ruled that members should not be called by any titles of privilege, but Anthony Lambton still insisted on being addressed as Lord Lambton. Now his title could not save him from a shamefaced retreat from Westminster.

Even as the ripples of Lambton's resignation spread 48 hours later, the reputation of another prominent politician was about to be shattered.

The Prime Minister had already ordered a full-scale inquiry into the other possible scandals uncovered by the Fleet Street journalists.

There was never any evidence to connect 55-year-old Lord Jellicoe, Lord Privy Seal and Leader of the House of Lords, with the drug-taking sexual orgies of prostitute Norma Levy and the furtive photographic sessions at her Maida Vale apartment. He appeared to have impeccable credentials for the most honourable of government appointments.

The son of a distinguished Admiral, he was a courageous war hero and a godson of King George V. As a dashing young colonel during World War II, he had won battle honours for his part in a sabotage attack on a German airfield in Crete and had been awarded the Military Cross for a parachute operation in Rhodes.

He was taken prisoner in 1943, and escaped to lead the force which liberated half of Greece, averted civil war and took control of Athens in just 22 days. He won the Légion d'Honneur from the French, and grateful Greece bestowed its own Military Cross on him.

In his career with the Foreign Office he had served in Washington, Brussels and Baghdad. Lord Jellicoe was a highly respected Leader of the House of Lords and far removed from Lambton's world of drug-taking and sexual practices.

But he did share the same kind of guilty secret in his liaisons with prostitutes.

He didn't wait for the invitation to appear before the investigators of Scotland Yard. Abruptly he submitted his resignation to Prime Minister Heath to spare the government the tedious embarrassment of uncovering his shame.

His letter to the prime minister admitted frankly:

When you told me yesterday that my name was being linked with allegations about a ring of call girls, I thought it right to tell you that unhappily there was justification for this because I had had some casual affairs which, if publicised, would be the subject of criticism.

It was almost too much for the presses of the popular newspapers to cope with — two senior politicians caught out in sexual scandal within days of each other, and the columns of the newspapers overflowing with juicy titbits and promising even more shocking revelations.

In Paris, the French Secret Service was ordered to update its files on the notorious brothel of 'Madame Claud' on Avenue Kleber, long noted for its diplomatic and political clientele. Sex sessions at the expensive house of pleasure were known to cost several hundred pounds a night, and it was feared that illustrious clients with state secrets might be open to blackmail.

In Germany, where commercial sex is legal, discreet observation was kept on two brothels in Frankfurt and Munich and several high-ranking politicians were warned of the dangers of availing themselves of the legitimate opportunities open to their fellow countrymen.

In Belgium a special squad of British and American investigators attached to the headquarters of NATO were assigned to check out the visitors to the brothels in Brussels pinpointed by the security services as 'diplomatic' venues for sex.

Back in London, the prime minister moved swiftly to organize a meeting of the Security Commission to examine the potential espionage loopholes in the cases of Lord Lambton and Lord Jellicoe. The commission, set up to examine breaches of security after the Profumo scandal, consisted of top judges, diplomats and civil servants.

Until the public disgrace of Lambton and Jellicoe hit the headlines, the commission had only investigated possible security risks and

Lord Jellicoe, former Lord Privy Seal

recommended changes in procedures as a result of the cases of convicted spies who had betrayed the nation's secrets to foreign powers.

While the commission began to gather its evidence, a series of

---

Unity Mitford

The extraordinary infatuation of an English aristocrat's daughter for the maniacal Adolf Hitler became a severe embarrassment for British officials in pre-war Berlin. Unity Mitford, daughter of Lord and Lady Redesdale, won her way into the Führer's inner circle, sat at his feet, prayed to his photograph and publicly averred that he was the new Messiah.

When her sister Diana married Sir Oswald Mosley, leader of the British Union of Fascists, Unity's fervour became even more intense. In Germany in 1935 and 1936 she spoke at Jew-baiting Nazi meetings led by Goebbels, Goering and the notorious Julius Streicher. She attended the Nuremberg rallies as Hitler's personal guest, on one occasion seated next to his mistress Eva Braun. In 1938 she was in Vienna to see Hitler's *Anschluss* celebrations after his march into Austria. Later that year he gave her a lavishly furnished Berlin apartment, recently vacated by a dispossessed Jewish family.

Such was the scandal at home in Britain that her father had to issue a statement to scotch talk of a romance with the Führer. It read: 'There has never been any question of an engagement between my daughter and Herr Hitler, who lives only for his country and has no time for marriage'.

Deprived of the protection of the British consul in Berlin and increasingly agitated by the prospect of war between her own country and her adopted fatherland, Unity closeted herself in her apartment and tuned in to every news bulletin. On 3 September 1939, when war was declared, she drove to the Interior Ministry, and handed in all her Nazi emblems along with a letter for Hitler. Then she strolled through Berlin's English Garden, put a gun to her temple and pulled the trigger.

The bullet lodged in her head, but Unity survived. Hitler visited her in hospital and paid all her medical bills. He allowed her parents into the country to take her home to Britain, where Home Secretary Herbert Morrison stated that her condition rendered her no risk to security.

Unity Mitford moved with her mother to a Hebridean island, where the bullet in her skull finally brought about her death. An abscess caused meningitis, and she died in the West Highland Cottage Hospital, Oban, in May 1948.

criminal cases in open courts sealed the fate of Lord Lambton and Colin and Norma Levy.

Lord Lambton pleaded guilty to two charges of possessing cannabis and amphetamines and was fined.

Colin Levy, who had fled with Norma to Spain, had quarrelled violently with her and had tried to run her down in a car as she walked through the narrow streets of the resort town of Denia. He was arrested by Spanish police and sent to prison.

Norma Levy returned to Britain of her own free will and admitted charges of controlling prostitutes. The charges never related to her meetings with Lord Lambton, but to her part in running a call-girl agency on behalf of women in a prostitution ring. She was fined £250.

When the Security Commission reported later that year, they were scathing in their condemnation of Lord Lambton's drug-taking.

The report warned:

He had admittedly on at least one occasion smoked cannabis when in the company of prostitutes in Norma Levy's flat. This is the soft drug which produces changes in mood and gives a feeling of irresponsibility. Recorded evidence existed of a conversation which suggested, whether correctly or not, his involvement with other drugs.

There was photographic evidence of sexual practices which deviated from normal. This evidence was in the hands of criminals and up for sale. Lord Lambton was thus wide open to blackmail.

We are wholly convinced that he would never betray his country's secrets. It is as inconceivable as in the case of Lord Jellicoe. The real risk lay in his use of cannabis. Under the influence of this drug we consider there would be significant danger of his divulging, without intention to do so, items of classified information of value to a foreign intelligence service. We do not suggest that Lord Lambton would consciously commit indiscretions in his normal state of mind but there is a risk he might do so in a mood of irresponsibility induced by drugs.

Norma Levy didn't wait around to hear the commission's findings. She returned to Spain, divorced her husband and married an American businessman. Later, when she moved to the United States, she was arrested and sent to jail on further prostitution charges. Her ex-husband Colin also moved to America, scraping a living as an odd-job man in the beach towns of Florida.

Lord Lambton left public life and moved away from his own wife and children to a self-imposed exile in a farmhouse in northern Italy. His career of politics and deception was over, and he was left to ponder the legend on the curse on the House of Lambton and the ironic warning of his own aristocratic family motto, *Le Jour Viendra . . . The Day will come.*

Cecil Parkinson

Cecil Parkinson was a man destined for the highest office in British politics. He was self-made, the highly acceptable face of capitalism, the brilliant mind which helped engineer Margaret Thatcher's election victory.

The scandal which then erupted over his love affair with his secretary Sara Keays — and which was played out in the full glare of publicity — was to have profound effects on the Conservative Party, to which he was dedicated. Not only did it wreck his career but it deprived the Cabinet of a brilliant tactician who was seen by many as the heir-apparent to the Iron Lady for the doorkey of No. 10 Downing Street.

Rumours of the Parkinson–Keays affair had been whispered in the halls of power for many months before it was splashed on to the front pages in October 1983.

The debonair Trade and Industry secretary, then 52, had enjoyed a passionate and secret affair with 36–year-old unmarried brunette Sara, a colonel's daughter, for ten years. She had fallen in love with him right from the start, and the illicit affair had blossomed into love — on both sides.

In 1979, when Parkinson was Trade Minister, he proposed to her . . . and she accepted. But it was an engagement without a ring or a wedding date. He told her that timing was all-important because of his marriage — and the rising political career which he could not afford to jeopardize.

It was an arrangement that both mistress and the unfaithful husband found suitable. The secret assignations, snatched moments alone and careful cover-ups were the prices paid to ensure that Parkinson's marriage to his wife Ann continued, and that his political career prospered.

In 1980 the affair cooled briefly when they agreed to slow the pace of the relationship. Sara left for a job in Brussels to work in the office of EEC supremo Roy Jenkins. Parkinson went on to become the Conservative Party chairman and close aide and confidant of Margaret Thatcher.

They were not apart for long. On her return to London the affair continued, with Sara nurturing the desire to one day become Mrs Parkinson.

By 9 June 1983, when the Conservatives romped home to victory in an election whose campaign was triumphantly managed by the man she loved, Sara was already nearly two months pregnant by him. Time was now running out for both the ill-fated affair and the glittering career of Cecil Parkinson.

Cecil Parkinson with his wife Anne outside their home

As the cheering crowds on polling day applauded Mrs Thatcher and her right-hand man, Sara Keays nurtured other thoughts. Her lover, she later claimed, had wanted to end the affair when she told him in May of the pregnancy. She also claimed that on polling day he had begged her for a reconciliation, with the pledge that he would divorce his wife and marry her. That was all she had ever wanted, she said.

Such indecision on the part of the usually decisive Cecil Parkinson was revealed only through the words of Miss Keays. When the affair broke in October that year, he made one statement on it, saying that would be all he ever would say about the matter. Unlike many statements made by politicians, he kept his word.

The affair could perhaps have been kept a discreet secret, but rumours began circulating to such an extent that the satirical magazine

Sara Keays, Cecil Parkinson's former secretary

Private Eye printed a story that she was expecting a child. It wasn't long before newspaper reporters were involved in a crazy car chase across London with Miss Keays as they attempted to question her about the identity of the father of her unborn child. Parkinson was being pushed into a corner from which there was no escape from publicity.

He dropped his bombshell on 5 October that year with a short statement through his solicitors which said:

To bring to an end rumour concerning Miss Sara Keays and myself, and to prevent further harassment of Miss Keays and her family, I wish, with her consent, to make the following statement.

I have had a relationship with Miss Keays over a number of years. She is expecting a child due to be born in January of whom I am the father. I am of course making financial provision for both mother and child.

During our relationship I told Miss Keays of my wish to marry her. Despite my having given Miss Keays that assurance, my wife, who has been a source of great strength, and I, decided to stay together and to keep our family together. I regret deeply the distress I have caused to Miss Keays, to her family and to my own family.

It created a political turmoil that ran on the front pages unabated. Reporters flocked to Sara Keays's home village of Marksbury, near Bath, to unearth every nugget of information possible on the mistress at the heart of this juicy scandal. Still more hordes waited on the doorstep of Mr Parkinson's family home in Hertfordshire to ask the vital question: would he resign?

Downing Street was adamant: 'The question of his resignation does not enter into it.' It looked as if in the face of a broiling political scandal, 'golden boy' Parkinson really was going to ride it out with his image intact, his family intact and his political career intact.

In fact he had just one week left before his political life was to collapse around him.

Both he and Sara had agreed on a pact of silence about the affair. He would make monetary provisions for the child, but the price on both sides was no further comment on the relationship.

But Sara was nurturing more, much more, than just hurt pride. She was the woman scorned, the mistress who gave the best years of her life for the man she loved because she believed his empty promises of marriage. When she saw Parkinson on the *Panorama* programme on Monday, 10 October — five days later — and he referred to her as 'the other person' — she played the trump card which ended his political life.

She drafted a long statement in *The Times*, which appeared the following Friday. The ten-point document stressed the dithering that Parkinson had had over whether or not to marry her, his broken promises and plans to divorce his wife. She ended the statement in Britain's most influential newspaper by saying:

Press comment, Government pronouncements and the continued speculation about this matter have put me in an impossible position. I feel that I have both a public duty and a duty to my family to put the record straight.

Cecil Parkinson was at the Imperial Hotel in Blackpool when he heard the news. The previous day he had received the tumultuous applause of the audience at the Conservative Party conference when he spoke — the endorsement of the faithful that he should stay. But after Sara's letter, there was nothing left for him but resignation. Following a three-minute meeting with Margaret Thatcher in the early hours of 14 October 1983, his career was finished. Sara Keays's statement had achieved that which public opinion had failed to do.

On New Year's Eve, Sara Keays gave birth to a healthy 8lb 3oz girl called Flora. It only remained for little Flora's father to wish her 'peace, privacy and a happy life'.

Edward VIII and Mrs Simpson

Edward VIII was King of England for 326 days before abandoning the throne for the woman he loved. The scandal came as a bolt from the blue to the British public, who hero-worshipped their new, handsome young king. It came as a savage shock to his shy, stuttering brother the Duke of York, who was forced unwillingly to take the throne in his stead. The only person it did not surprise was Wallis Simpson, an American divorcée.

Edward met Wallis when he was still Prince of Wales and she was married to her second husband, Ernest Simpson. She was slender and sophisticated, and captivated him. Before the death of his father King George V, Edward jaunted around Europe with his new love.

The entire world knew about the prince's mistress — except for the British public. While newspapers around the globe published countless stories of the couple's romance, all were clipped by censors before going on sale in Britain. And the British press breathed not a word.

The Duke later admitted that he had decided to marry Wallis as early as 1934. Yet it was not until 3 December 1936 that the affair became public knowledge. He abdicated on the 11th.

The great conspiracy of silence was broken, ironically, by a man who knew nothing of the matter. Dr Blunt, Bishop of Bradford, publicly criticized what seemed to be the new king's playboy lifestyle. Those in the know assumed him to be talking about the Wallis Simpson affair, and Fleet Street broke the story it had been sitting on for years.

The next few days were hell for Wallis. The windows of her home in London's Cumberland Terrace were shattered by stones. Letters and telegrams and abuse flowed in.

Her divorce, which had gone through quietly at Ipswich, Suffolk, a few weeks earlier, came under fresh investigation. Her husband had allowed himself to be divorced for adultery, supposedly committed at a Thames-side hotel with a lady named 'Buttercup' Kennedy. One American paper had headlined the divorce case 'King's Moll Reno-ed'. But the British press had given it only a couple of paragraphs.

Wallis was terrified of the public reaction and fled to the south of France. 'I didn't know it would be like this,' she said.

The coronation of Edward VIII was not due until May, and the king still believed that his immense popularity would allow him to swing public opinion in time to make Wallis his queen. He reckoned without the implacable opposition of Prime Minister Stanley Baldwin.

When Edward had declared his love for Wallis to his mother, Queen Mary, the old lady had angrily sent for Baldwin. He immediately sought an audience with the lovestruck Edward and told him: 'People are talking about you and this American woman. I have had so many nasty letters from people who respected your father and do not like the way you are going on.'

Baldwin realized that the country faced a grave constitutional crisis — but he could not help being impressed by the obvious sincerity of the king's love for his mistress. He spoke later of Edward's 'exalted state of mind'. He said: 'The king's face bore such a look of beauty as might have lighted the face of a young knight who had caught a glimpse of the Holy Grail.'

The royal family were unimpressed, however. And they were less than amused by the nickname American newspapers had given to Wallis . . . 'Queen Wally'.

Queen Mary tried to talk the king into putting duty before love. Later she wrote to him: 'You did not seem able to take in any point of view save your own.'

The king was surprised to find he had an ally in Winston Churchill. At the height of the crisis, Churchill said at lunch: 'Why shouldn't the king marry his cutie?' But Noel Coward, who was at the same table, reflected the feelings of the British people. 'Because,' he said, 'England does not want a Queen Cutie.'

In November 1935, before the scandal broke, a way of allowing the king to marry Wallis and stay on the throne had been suggested by newspaper magnate Esmond Harmsworth, later Lord Rothermere. Over lunch at Claridges Hotel he had put to Wallis the idea of a morganatic marriage. This would have meant that she would become the king's wife but not his queen, and that children of the marriage would have no claim to the throne.

Wallis said the idea was inhuman. But the king was desperate to make public his love for her, and he asked Harmsworth to put the idea to the prime minister. The Cabinet met secretly to discuss the proposal — and rejected it unanimously.

By the eighth day of the crisis the king had shut himself away at his country home, Fort Belvedere, near Virginia Water, Surrey. He spent most of the time on the telephone to Wallis, who was in Cannes.

The American divorcée had little understanding of the British constitution or the country's traditions. She had had no idea that her love for the king could cause such a storm. She told him that she was prepared to make a statement renouncing any claims on him. The king would have none of it.

Later that day Baldwin read the abdication statement to the House of Commons. The following night the king broadcast to the nation from Windsor Castle, explaining why he had abdicated. His last words

The Duke and Duchess of Windsor on their wedding day

were: 'God bless you all and God save the king.' By 'the king' he meant his brother George.

Edward, under his new title Duke of Windsor, then left Britain by Royal Navy destroyer to join the woman he loved, never to set foot on his native soil again.

It was Christmas time, and in the streets children were singing:

Hark! The Herald Angels sing,
Mrs Simpson's pinched our king.

They were married in the town of Condé, near Tours, France, and it was in that country that they settled. The city of Paris provided them with a vast white château, for which they paid £3 a week, and they lived there, apart from a wartime break, for 35 years until the Duke's death on 28 May 1972 at the age of 77.

Only then was he again honoured by his own country. For two days he lay in state at St George's Chapel, Windsor, and 57,903 people filed past his body to pay their respects.

For the first time in her life the Duchess of Windsor stayed at Buckingham Palace then, on the night of Saturday, 3 June, she was driven to Windsor. There she was met by Prince Charles and Lord Mountbatten, who accompanied her into the candle-lit chapel after it had been closed to the public. Pale, slim, dressed in black, she spent eight minutes behind the catafalque of her husband. It was her 35th wedding anniversary.

She read the messages on some of the hundreds of floral tributes. One attached to a spray of flowers read: 'To the dear memory of our late king, the Duke of Windsor, who threw hypocrisy to the winds and committed himself to the brotherhood of man, and who is loved beyond measure.'

Then the woman who was born Bessie Wallis Warfield in Baltimore in 1896, who came to Britain and stole a king, and who was shunned throughout her life as a result, returned home to Paris to spend the rest of her lonely days bedridden from a debilitating disease.

Within reach, on the table of her dressing room, stood a framed message in the Duke of Windsor's own handwriting:

My friend, with thee to live alone,
Methinks were better than to own
A crown, a sceptre and a throne.

Princess Margaret

It was wartime and there was much to be serious about. But not for a vivacious teenage princess with all the excitement of life and love ahead of her. The Royal Family's apartments at Buckingham Palace rang with young Margaret's laughter and joyful chatter. 'I'm so lucky to be me,' she would tell her friends.

She was a very pretty, slightly precocious girl, spoiled by her father King George VI, who doted on her. Fully aware of her appeal, she flirted outrageously.

In 1944 came the event that was to change her life. Group Captain Peter Townsend, a handsome, debonair 29-year-old RAF war hero, was taken on to the king's staff as Extra Air Equerry. Margaret was infatuated from the moment her father introduced him to her. She said later: 'Peter appeared when I was 14. I had a terrific crush on him.'

The king was once heard to remark that he would have liked a son

Princess Margaret leaving Mansion House, March 1955

like Townsend. The new equerry was married and lived with his wife Rosemary in the grounds of Windsor Castle. No one took much notice of the increasing time Margaret spent with the good-looking young officer. It was, after all, only a schoolgirl crush, and the older man would be a steadying influence on her.

But that first, wild infatuation was to become a poignant love story that would divide the royal family, and rock the nation. . . .

After the war, Prince Philip of Greece arrived on the scene, and began courting Margaret's sister Elizabeth. But there was little love between him and Townsend. Philip, a bluff, hearty 'man's man', had almost nothing in common with the quietly spoken, debonair and dry-witted RAF officer.

In 1947 King George wanted to test the strength of feeling between Philip and Elizabeth, so he parted them by taking the royal family on a three-month tour of South Africa. For Elizabeth and her beau three months of parting was a lifetime.

But Margaret, now nearly 17, was overjoyed at the prospect of the trip. For Townsend would be going while his wife stayed at home. The romantic voyage seemed to her more like a honeymoon, and it was during the tour that her crush on this man twice her age developed into a deeper, lasting love. But he was married and her father's right-hand man. There was no possibility of an involvement . . . yet.

Philip waited patiently for Elizabeth's return, and they married in November 1947.

Margaret, certain that Townsend would be hers one day, passed her time with a bunch of rich, amusing young people — the so-called 'Princess Margaret set'. Leading lights included the late Billy Wallace and the Hon. Colin Tennant, who was later to give her a plot of land on his island of Mustique.

Townsend's marriage went on the rocks in 1951. It had begun with a wartime romance, the wedding a snatched moment during a brief leave in 1941. His RAF duties and, later, his royal commitments, meant lengthy separations.

Townsend, by this time Deputy Master of the Royal Household, talked to the king about his marital problems and it was decided he should quietly divorce his wife for her adultery with Johnny de Laszlo.

On 14 August 1951, four days before Margaret's 21st birthday, she was out riding with Townsend in the wooded grounds of Balmoral when he told her of his coming divorce. At last Margaret could see her dreams beginning to come true.

The princess's close relationship with the king's aide was already the talk of the palace, though not a whisper had reached the public. The king was angry when he came across Townsend carrying Margaret in his arms up a flight of stairs. Margaret said: 'I asked him to carry me, papa. I ordered him to.'

With Townsend's marriage officially doomed, they were soon spending every spare moment together. They would drive away from the palace in a plain car for quiet evenings at the homes of trusted friends.

Margaret was heartbroken when her father, whom she adored, died in February 1952. At his funeral the card on her wreath read: 'Darling papa, from his everloving Margaret.'

Townsend's divorce came through in the following December, and now the princess was sure nothing could possibly stand in their way. Except officialdom.

To set her mind at rest she asked Sir Alan Lascelles, then the Queen's private secretary, if it would be possible for her to marry a man who had been what was then called the 'innocent party' in a divorce. He told her it would be possible after a suitable time had elapsed. She was overjoyed.

After Elizabeth acceded to the throne, Margaret and her mother moved out of the palace into Clarence House. She asked Townsend, now the Queen's equerry, to help her choose the colour schemes for her quarters, in the belief that one day he would share them. The couple were taking less care to hide their romance. Often they would slip away separately from official functions, meet nearby and go to the cinema or a friend's house.

Prince Philip, however, who was still strongly anti-Townsend, was urging officials to have him moved — out of range of his sister-in-law.

First rumours of Margaret's secret love were leaking out during the build-up to the coronation in June 1953. And it was the princess who finally gave the game away after the Westminster Abbey ceremony.

As she talked excitedly to Townsend, she leaned forward to brush a loose thread from his uniform. It was the simple, caring gesture of a woman in love. One reporter noticed and saw the group captain hold out his hands to her. He said Margaret seemed about to fall into his arms.

Next day their romance was the talk of the nation's breakfast tables. Palace officials were horrified. Here were the makings of another royal scandal only 17 years after the abdication crisis had shaken the monarchy. Then, Winston Churchill had been heavily attacked for taking the side of Edward VIII and Mrs Simpson. Now, as prime minister, he acted quickly to separate the lovers. Townsend was given the job of air attaché in Brussels, and Margaret and her mother were despatched on a tour of Rhodesia.

Privately, the devoted couple were told they must wait a year, and they agreed to what they believed was a temporary parting. Margaret is reported to have said: 'We were given to believe we could marry eventually.'

The princess telephoned Townsend from Africa twice a day, and

Group Captain Peter Townsend arriving for Air Ministry talks

they planned their farewell tryst before he left for Brussels. But Townsend was given orders to report for duty in Belgium the day before Margaret was due back. She was furious.

She shut out the pain with an endless round of nightclubbing and partying with the Margaret set.

Townsend was told his one-year posting would be stretched to two years, then to nearly three. Every time his return was delayed, Margaret was told the time was 'not ripe'. There were only snatched moments of bliss when Townsend was able to slip back to England. But Margaret still believed that one day they would be in each other's arms with the blessing of Church and State.

Then, as her 25th birthday approached, the Cabinet made the decision that was to shatter her dreams.

Parliament could never approve her marriage to the divorced Townsend, she was told. If she married without approval, she would have to give up her royal status and privileges, and might be ordered into exile, like her uncle the Duke of Windsor.

Churchill sent the bewildered princess off on another tour, to the Caribbean, knowing it was a part of the world she longed to visit. He hoped the lavish, no-expense-spared hospitality and superb organization of a royal tour would rub home to Margaret all she would be giving up by marrying Townsend.

Even at that late stage, the determined princess was sure she could make officialdom relent. Privately, the Queen was on her side. But there was a strong anti-Townsend faction in the palace, led by Prince Philip. Outside there was opposition from the Cabinet, the Church and Commonwealth leaders.

The lovers did not stand a chance.

On Wednesday, 12 October 1955 the scene was set and the cast were taking up their positions for the last act of the doomed romance. Margaret arrived in London on a night train from Scotland, where she had been holidaying at Balmoral. She went straight to Clarence House. Townsend made an early start to drive from Brussels to Le Touquet, where he caught the air ferry to Lydd, Kent. After driving to a friend's London home and unpacking, he went to Clarence House and spent two hours with the woman he loved.

The couple were heartened by the support of the British public. As Townsend left Clarence House there were shouts of: 'Good luck, sir!' from the crowd which had gathered outside. And when Margaret drove through the East End of London, women shouted: 'Go on, marry him!'

On Friday, 14 October the couple went to Berkshire to spend the weekend with friends. That evening there was a champagne dinner. They returned to London separately on Monday, but dined together in the evening.

Still hoping the Cabinet would relent in the face of public opinion, Margaret and Townsend passed the next seven days waiting and praying, and spending as much time as possible together.

But on Tuesday, 25 October they realized they had lost the battle. The years of waiting had been wasted. They would never marry. Margaret told the Queen and the Archbishop of Canterbury the next morning, and that evening she and Townsend got hopelessly drunk at a dinner party with friends in Knightsbridge, London.

They drafted a statement the following day and an approved version was released on Monday, 31 October. With moving simplicity, it read:

I would like it to be known that I have decided not to marry Group Captain Peter Townsend. I have been aware that subject to my renouncing my rights of succession it might have been possible for me to contract a civil marriage. But mindful of the Church's teaching that a Christian marriage is indissoluble and conscious of my duty to the Commonwealth, I have resolved to put these considerations before any others. I have reached the decision entirely alone, and in doing so I have been strengthened by the unfailing support and devotion of Group Captain Townsend. I am grateful for the concern of all those who have constantly prayed for my happiness.

Townsend quit his Brussels post and set off on an 18-month round-the-world trip, taking a team that included a young Belgian girl, Marie-Luce, who looked remarkably like Princess Margaret. They later married and settled near Paris, where they raised three children.

Margaret sought forgetfulness with her set. She was unofficially engaged briefly to Billy Wallace, but they broke up in a blazing row after he had a fling with another girl in Nassau.

It was at the wedding of another former suitor, Colin Tennant, that she met the man destined to take the place of Townsend in her heart . . . Taking the pictures was a rising young photographer, Anthony Armstrong-Jones.

It was not love at first sight at that initial meeting in 1956, but the gentle, sensitive young man caught the princess's eye when they were both invited to a dinner party.

Soon Margaret was happier and more relaxed than she had been for years. When she visited Tony's scruffy studio in London's docklands she could forget the conventions that usually bound her. As she spent more and more time with her man of the moment her royal engagements suffered. Friends tried to warn both parties of the dangers, but they were obviously very much in love.

Their engagement was announced in February 1960, and on 6 May they had a fairytale wedding at Westminster Abbey.

At the start of the sixties, life was kind to the princess and Lord Snowdon (as he now was). Two children were born. But that early happiness did not last. Their temperaments pulled them apart.

Lord Snowdon's barber, who visited their Kensington Palace home frequently, told later how he had witnessed several royal flare-ups — including one in which Margaret slammed a mirrored door so fiercely that it shattered into fragments.

A major row developed over Tony's decision to buy and renovate a country cottage in Sussex. He went off to Japan without making up the quarrel. The princess was so upset that she became ill and went into hospital.

Tony denied there was a rift between them, and they took a 10-day holiday to try to work things out. They failed.

A new pattern emerged. Margaret would take holidays alone while Tony would spend more and more time at his cottage, often visiting his neighbour the Marquis of Reading, who had a very pretty daughter, Lady Jacqueline Rufus Isaacs. Soon Tony and Jacqueline were meeting regularly — a friendship which became known to the public and the Palace, who put pressure on Snowdon to end it.

More and more, the royal couple's private squabbles were spilling over into their public lives. . . .

At a charity ball Snowdon spent most of the evening dancing with the same girl. Margaret watched their every movement. Then, during an interlude, she walked over to the girl and asked sweetly: 'Are you enjoying yourself?'

'Very much so, ma'am,' she replied.

The smile left Margaret's face and her eyes narrowed. 'That's enough for one evening, then,' she said coldly. 'Run along home!' The girl went.

On one occasion Margaret is said to have burst into Tony's study when he was discussing a work project with a colleague. He flew into a rage and shouted: 'Never come in here without knocking!'

When he took her to dinner in London one evening he also took along a portable television and put it on the table. He made no attempt at conversation and instead watched Harold Wilson explaining Britain's economic problems.

By now Margaret had established her own court on the island of Mustique in the West Indies. Colin Tennant had given her a plot of land there as a wedding present and she built herself a holiday hideaway home. Tony never visited it.

It was through the Tennants that Margaret met the man who innocently caused the final fragile ties of the marriage to be broken.

Apart from holidaying on Colin Tennant's island of Mustique, Margaret would travel north every September to join a house party at the landowner's Scottish seat. In 1973 the party was one short at the last moment. Tennant invited an aquaintance of his aunt to make up the numbers. His name was Roddy Llewellyn.

The atmosphere between Margaret and Roddy was charged from

Princess Margaret at the Theatre Royal, London, 1984

the moment they were introduced. They spent much time chatting together.

After that Margaret and Roddy, 17 years her junior, would meet in London and at the homes of their friends. They introduced each other to completely opposite lifestyles. Llewellyn stayed on a commune in an old farmhouse in the west of England. When Margaret visited she wore old clothes and looked, in the words of a villager, like a farmer's wife.

The secret friendship became stronger. Roddy, the handsome, sensitive son of a baronet, looked like a younger version of Lord Snowdon. But he had not the demanding, fiery temperament of the princess's husband. Roddy's perfect — and publicly deferential — manners appealed to Margaret.

In March 1974 the couple spent a blissful holiday at the princess's villa on Mustique. Colin Tennant turned journalists away at the airport, and not a word of the couple's romance appeared in the newspapers. But while they were away Snowdon celebrated his 44th birthday at a London restaurant, and the press noted the absence of his wife.

Late in 1974 Margaret and Tony made a new attempt to save their marriage. The princess told Roddy that their affair had to end.

Llewellyn was heartbroken. He flew to Barbados to stay at a house his family owned. He found it empty. Shortly afterwards he collapsed and was flown back to Britain with a doctor at his side.

Meanwhile Snowdon had gone to Australia to make a television series. The production assistant was Lucy Lindsay-Hogg, the attractive daughter of an Irish clothing manufacturer. Her marriage to film director Michael Lindsay-Hogg had ended four years earlier.

Margaret knew nothing about their burgeoning friendship, and when

Roddy Llewellyn returning from a holiday in Mustique with Princess Margaret

her husband returned home from Australia she welcomed him warmly, hoping that this time they could make the marriage work. But it soon became clear that the rift was too deep.

In March 1976 Margaret flew to Mustique for another holiday, and this time a journalist managed to get on to the island with a camera. The following Sunday a photograph appeared on the front page of the *News of the World* in Britain. It showed Princess Margaret and Roddy Llewellyn sitting in swimsuits and sipping drinks at a beachfront bar.

The photograph, the first of the couple together, sparked a worldwide sensation. Revelations about Margaret's visits to the farm commune were dredged up. Newspapers spoke of her 'life among the hippies' and suggested that some other visitors to the remote farm had had a fondness for marijuana. A member of parliament described the princess as 'a wayward woman' in the House of Commons.

The stories could no longer be contained and the Queen realized that the true situation had to be spelled out to the world. On 19 March Kensington Palace released a statement beginning: 'HRH the Princess Margaret, the Countess of Snowdon, and the Earl of Snowdon have mutually agreed to live apart. . . .'

Lord Snowdon was on another trip to Australia when the announcement was made. He went on television and tearfully appealed for his children's understanding. He wished his wife happiness in the future, and declared his admiration for the royal family.

There were no more statements, no kiss-and-tell revelations. Lord Snowdon never again spoke publicly about those turbulent years at Kensington Palace. Roddy Llewellyn, the perfect English gentleman, never told his side of the story that rocked royalty.

A divorce in 1978 left Tony free to wed the new girl in his life, Lucy Lindsay-Hogg. Roddy went on to find his own beautiful bride, Tatiana Soskin. Both couples soon had new families to fill their lives.

Princess Margaret remained alone.

Music-loving Princess Margaret was determined to make a success of a trip to North America to raise money for London's Royal Opera House, Covent Garden. At first everyone was charmed by the princess, and she shone at champagne receptions. Then a journalist claimed that she had called the Irish 'pigs'. Few people accepted the hasty denials, or the explanation that any epithet would have been aimed only at the terrorists responsible for the murder of the Earl Mountbatten, the royal family's beloved 'Uncle Dickie'. Cheers turned to jeers, and Margaret's life was even threatened. It was reported that only daily telephone calls from Roddy Llewellyn helped her to go on smiling.

CHAPTER 2

All That Glitters

Rock Stars
Elvis Presley
Fatty Arbuckle
Charlie Chaplin
Marilyn Monroe

Lana Turner
Sarah Miles
Koo Stark
Marvin Gaye

Rock Stars

Sex, drugs and booze punctuate the story of rock and roll . . . and the lives of the wild men and women who make the music. Scandal after scandal has erupted around supergroups like the Rolling Stones and the Beatles. And many stars have been destroyed by their crazy life-styles . . . like Rolling Stone Brian Jones, The Who's Keith Moon, Janis Joplin, Jimi Hendrix and Billie Holliday. The 'King' himself, Elvis Presley, fell victim, and his story is told in the next chapter.

For years the Rolling Stones ruled as the greatest rock and roll band in the world, and to their screaming girl fans the sexiest Stone of all was the pouting, prancing Mick Jagger.

There has been a long procession of beautiful women in his life. There was Chrissie Shrimpton, then 17, sister of top sixties model Jean 'The Shrimp' Shrimpton. The relationship foundered because Jagger made her stay in the background, believing steady girlfriends were bad for the group's image.

Then came singer Marianne Faithfull, also 17 when they met at a party. Jagger, who had been ignoring Chrissie at his side, yawned, stood up and walked across to where Marianne was sitting. 'I'm Mick Jagger,' he said. Then he quite deliberately poured his glass of champagne down the front of her shirt. He mumbled a vague apology in the cockney accent he often adopted and began to mop the spilled drink with his hands, slowly and pointedly.

Marianne stood up, almost knocking him over, and walked away. She was heard to say loudly: 'He's a dreadful, spotty slob. I hate pimply men and he's got more spots on his face than I've ever seen.' They next met in a recording studio where Marianne was to record her hit *As Tears Go By*, written by Jagger. Slowly she was being drawn into the Stones' world.

'I wanted to be an actress and a scholar,' she said later. 'But whatever I did I wanted to be great at it. My first move was to get a Rolling Stone as a boyfriend. I slept with three of them and decided the lead singer was the best bet.'

Mick Jagger and Marianne Faithfull arriving at the Royal Opera House

Separated from her husband of a year, John Dunbar, she set up home with Jagger in London's Chelsea in 1967 and rapidly lost her sweet schoolgirl image when she featured in the drugs trial involving Jagger and fellow Stone Keith Richards as the outrageous Miss X who, wearing nothing but a fur rug, was the centrepiece of an orgy allegedly interrupted by the police raid. Jagger and Richards were convicted and imprisoned, but released in the face of public opposition to what was widely regarded as harassment.

The stories at the time — of drugs, wild parties and kinky sex — seemed the more scandalous because Marianne looked so young and innocent. They called her The Angel With Soiled Wings. In 1969 she took a drug overdose and ended up in a coma in a Sydney hospital. The following year she parted from Jagger, who embarked on a passionate affair with black singer Marsha Hunt, star of the sixties musical *Hair*. A daughter, Karis, was born in 1970 and more scandal surrounded Jagger with a lengthy paternity battle. In 1979 a Los Angeles court ruled that he was the father and ordered him to pay upkeep. Marianne says: 'If Marsha had gone to Mick quietly about money for their daughter he would have given it to her. But she dragged it through the courts and the newspapers. That sort of thing really angers Mick. He feels exploited.'

Wherever the Stones went there were hordes of groupies — girls whose only ambition was to have sex with their idols. Mike Gruber, a former Stones manager, says: 'Every time Jagger and Richards went out there would be lots of chicks. I never saw them speak to a dame and say hello or ask them if they wanted a drink or any of the usual pleasantries. The girls were there for the taking and at the end of the evening it would be, "You — come with me." That was the extent of the conversation.'

In 1970 Jagger met Nicaraguan beauty Bianca. Commenting on the remarkable resemblance between Jagger and herself, Bianca once said: 'When Mick saw me for the first time he had a shock. He thought he was looking at himself. People love to theorize that Mick thought it would be amusing to marry his twin, but I want to be frank. He wanted to achieve the ultimate in sexual experience by making love to himself.'

They married in 1971 at St Tropez. Bianca, four months pregnant, was not able to fit into the wedding gown designed for her by Ossie Clark. Instead she wore a white St Laurent suit, slashed open to the waist, and far from the decorous modesty expected of a bride. She gave birth to a daughter, Jade, in October.

Bianca was not prepared to be just a mother and housewife. She became a top model and a London celebrity. Pictures of her were in all the glossy magazines. One fashion journal breathlessly told its readers: 'She wears no underwear, just tights, and her nipples are shaped like rosebuds.'

Bianca Jagger

Shortly before Jagger and Bianca parted in 1977 the Stones were once again at the centre of a scandal, over a controversial sex and drugs movie. The band had asked documentary film producer Robert Frank to make a film about their 1972 tour of South America. It was intended to be for public showing, but the scenes of sexual activity and drug-taking were allegedly so explicit that Jagger decided it should not be screened.

There was said to have been a long sequence of sky-high sex with members of the Stones' entourage making love to groupies at 30,000ft in a jet crossing America. One person was seen having a playful struggle with a full-breasted teenage girl. One couple made love in the space between two seats while a stewardess walked past unconcerned with a tray of drinks. Two of the group were seen watching a nude couple have sex as they provided a musical accompaniment on tambourines and maracas.

Frank said: 'When the plane was making its landing approach one couple were still making love. The guy took his girl, still naked, on his lap and fastened the seat belt around both of them.' The late Truman Capote, the American author, who was also on the plane, said: 'The couple made love in every imaginable position.'

Jagger caused yet more shock waves in 1978 with a line in his song *Some Girls*. There were angry protests over the words 'Black women like to fuck all night.' Dismissing the complaints, he said the song was dedicated to two African girls he met in Paris. 'We made love all night then they came to the studio with me. We were tired out and I made up the song on the spur of the moment.'

Jagger's stormy marriage to Bianca finally crumbled when he met six-foot Texan model Jerry Hall in 1978. Jerry described her Stone as 'the sexiest man in the world and the best lover ever', without perhaps fully realizing that his was a skill born of constant practice.

She was widely reputed to have tamed him and turned him into a one-woman man. But Jagger wasn't ready to give up his wild ways so readily. It was to teach him a lesson that Jerry had her much-publicized affair with millionaire Robert Sangster in 1983.

She revealed that she got mad when she kept finding other women's hairpins and ear-rings in his bed. She said it was not long before Jagger was soon on the phone begging her to come home.

He did not like the tables being turned. 'It was very silly of Jerry,' he told newspapers. 'And it was stupid to flaunt it in all the papers.' He admitted he enjoyed 'casual affairs if they came along' but said he was much more discreet than she was. He added that he was now so happy with Jerry, the mother of his daughter Elizabeth Scarlett and son James Leroy, that he had given up other women.

'I can be faithful despite what some people say,' he said in 1985. 'But I don't know how long for. I've been faithful for more than a year but I don't think I've ever been faithful for more than two years. I think when you go on the road you kind of let things like being faithful go to pieces. If you have a strong relationship you can usually get over that kind of ten-minute fling.

'I think it's almost inevitable in a long relationship that one or both partners is unfaithful. But as long as it can be made up afterwards it's fine. I think the constant bickering you see between some couples is far worse than a quick one in some hotel in Arkansas or somewhere. At least when I look back on my life I can say I've tried it all. I've been faithful and I've been unfaithful. I've tried this and I've tried that. There won't be much I've missed out on.'

Jagger's fellow Stone Keith Richards has been at the centre of scandal more often than any other member of the band. In 1967 he was found guilty of allowing people to smoke hashish at his Sussex home. His one-year jail sentence was quashed on appeal.

In 1973 he was fined £500 and given a one-year sentence for drug offences in France. That same year he was fined £205 in Britain for possessing drugs and for having arms and ammunition without a licence. Four years later he was fined £750 with £250 costs by a British court for possessing cocaine. It was found in a silver sniffing tube on the floor of his Bentley after it had crashed on the M1.

Then, one Sunday afternoon in 1977 in Toronto, Royal Canadian Mounted Police burst into his hotel room. He was in bed, and his girlfriend, former German model Anita Pallenberg, was in the room. The Mounties claimed they found an ounce of heroin and an ounce and a half of cocaine. Only a week earlier Anita had been fined £200 after pleading guilty to possessing drugs at Toronto airport.

Richards was charged with trafficking — which carried a maximum sentence of life imprisonment — and lived on a knife edge of suspense for 18 months before his trial. But after hearing that he and Anita were undergoing treatment for their addiction, the judge let him go free, on condition he give a charity concert for the blind.

He and Anita had first sought medical help for their drug problem in 1972, when they were expecting their second child and were worried that the baby could be born an addict. Happily their daughter, Dandelion, was a healthy baby with no addiction.

Looking back on his years of addiction to heroin, Richards said: 'I've been through the furnace and out the other side. Whether you have millions or whether you've got nothing, heroin is the great equalizer. I used to have to go down to Manhattan's lower East Side to score. It's as bad as it can be down there. I'd be carrying a shooter in my pocket. Nothing mattered except getting the dope.'

The couple's 12-year relationship ended in a blaze of scandal in 1979 after a headline-grabbing tragedy while Richards was in Paris making a record. Anita's 17-year-old lover, high-school dropout Scott Cantrell, shot himself dead as he sat on her bed at the Richards' home just outside New York.

Anita was the girl who rolled from Stone to Stone. First there was the tragic Brian Jones, the wildest of them all, who drowned in his swimming pool. Two years later, while she was living with Richards, she had a wild fling with Jagger when they co-starred in the film *Performance*. Actor James Fox, who was in the film, was shocked to find them making love in Jagger's dressing room during a ten-minute break from shooting.

Jones had founded the Stones, with Jagger and Richards, and was the original leader. The wildest Stone of all, he cut a flamboyant, dandified figure, and the girls lusted for him. They would be waiting in his bathroom, in his wardrobe and in his bed, and he took them two at a time. He once kept count of the women he had in one month and reached a total of 67. He fathered six illegitimate children by six women.

But as the Stones' fame grew he gradually lost his place in the limelight to Jagger. For him it was the beginning of the end. He turned to cocaine, heroin and whisky to ease the pain and became increasingly unreliable. He would arrive late for rehearsals or not at all. Then the two harshest blows struck him in quick succession. Girlfriend Anita Pallenberg left him for Richards, and in June 1969 he was dropped from the group.

On 3 July, at the age of 26, he was pulled unconscious from the pool of his country home. His new girlfriend, a nurse, tried to revive him until an ambulance arrived but Jones was beyond saving. Had he meant to take his life? Had he suffered an asthma attack? Or was he too high on drink or drugs to save himself when he got into difficulties?

He took the answer to his grave, leaving a self-penned epitaph that was read at his funeral: 'Please don't judge me too harshly.'

If the Stones at first set the pace for scandal and hell-raising, others were catching up fast. Like Keith Moon, who as drummer with supergroup The Who had reached the very pinnacles of rock success. But on the morning of 7 September 1978 he cooked himself a steak breakfast, ate it and then swallowed a fatal dose of more than 30 sleeping tablets.

Whether or not he chose to die remains a mystery, but since divorcing his wife Kim three years earlier he had seemed hellbent on a trail of self-destruction. His friends were brandy, champagne and girls whose names he seldom remembered. His legendary antics included flushing dynamite down hotel lavatories and dressing up in Nazi uniform to taunt his jetset neighbours in California. He was thrown off a British Airways jet two months before he died after trying to break into the flight deck to play his drumsticks on the instrument panel.

The day before he died he proposed to his girlfriend, Swedish beauty Annette Walter-Lax. That night they had danced together at a London showbusiness party and Moon was talking enthusiastically about his role in the forthcoming Monty Python film *The Life Of Brian*. The couple left the party to see the film *The Buddy Holly Story*. Perhaps the reminder of Buddy's death in an air crash struck some kind of chord with him.

His doctor told the inquest that Moon considered his sleeping tablets to be fairly harmless. The coroner said there was no evidence of a deliberate overdose and returned an open verdict.

With Jimi Hendrix the path to annihilation followed the well-trodden rock route of booze, drugs and wild living. He discovered the two passions 'that were to dominate his life, music and sex, before he was in his teens. At the age of nine he was given a guitar by an uncle and took to it enthusiastically.

He said his first experience of sex was at the age of 12. At 15 he was expelled from school after cheeking a teacher who ticked him off for holding a girl's hand in class.

After a spell as a paratrooper in the US Army, Hendrix drifted from town to town and band to band, playing guitar with whoever would have him but failing to make a big impression. In 1966 he moved to London, and in Britain he swiftly found the success that had eluded him in America. He formed his band, the Experience, who for two years were dominant figures on the rock concert circuit.

Hendrix was one of rock's wild men: his violent stage antics were often more anger than showmanship. At the end of one concert he set fire to his guitar and said afterwards: 'Me and this guitar had been in spiritual conflict all evening. I told it to do one thing and it did another. I wanted to kill it. I was ready to tear it apart with my bare hands.'

Once he was jailed in Sweden for smashing up an hotel room. But the morning after he could remember nothing of the incident. A girlfriend, Cathy Etchingham, recalled: 'One moment he would be quiet and gentle and the next moment he would smash up a room, no matter whose house he was in, and hit anyone who interfered, man or woman.' His downhill run gathered speed after the Experience broke up in November 1968 to the disappointment of their millions of fans.

In his final years he was in an almost permanent drugged daze and would drink two bottles of whisky at a sitting. He was 27 when he died in London after taking an overdose of his girlfriend's sleeping pills on 18 September 1970. There was no evidence that he was trying to commit suicide, and the coroner returned an open verdict.

Janis Joplin's tragedy was that she hated her looks. She had been a pretty, cherub-faced, fair-haired child, but in puberty she developed acne, which left her face permanently scarred. Her hair turned brown and uncontrollable and she put on weight.

Jimmy Hendrix

She was badly hurt when other kids nicknamed her 'Pig' at school. She took up with a gang of hooligans and began drinking beer heavily. She went to university but dropped out after only a year when fellow students nominated her 'Ugliest Man on the Campus'. She tried to pretend she didn't care about the taunts by dressing drably, having unkempt hair and never wearing make-up. But the truth was she cared dreadfully.

She soon turned to drugs. 'I was just a young chick, I wanted to get it on,' she said later. 'I wanted to smoke dope, take dope, lick dope, suck dope, fuck dope, anything I could lay my hands on I wanted to do it, man.'

Janis sought release from her unloved appearance in music — and drink and drugs gave her the courage to go on stage. Up there she was a new, brash, confident personality. Gone were her shapeless old garments. In their place were feathers, beads and sexy dresses. Sometimes she would come on in a mini skirt with silver high-heeled boots and black net stockings.

'Stomping and posing like an imperious whore, stroking her mike and whipping her hair around,' as one critic wrote, she could drive her audience to a frenzy before singing a word. But she couldn't do it without the whisky and the heroin.

She would drink a whole bottle of Southern Comfort during her act, and once said: 'When I get scared or worried I just say, "Janis, have a good time." I juice up real good and that's just what I have. I'd rather have ten years of super hypermost than live to be 70 sitting in some goddam chair watching television.'

In private she was desperately lonely. After one concert she said sadly: 'I just made love to 25,000 people and I'm going home alone.' She went for one-night stands with young boys — and girls — and when they weren't around there was always the bottle. When she heard of Hendrix's death, she said: 'Goddam it. He beat me to it.' Janis died less than three weeks later, of an overdose of heroin, on 4 October 1970. Like Hendrix, she was 27.

Scandal was a constant companion for beautiful blues singer Billie Holliday, who battled against her addiction to heroin and alcohol for most of her adult life . . . and finally lost.

She was born Eleanora Fagan when her mother Sadie Fagan was just 13 and a hospital cleaner. Her father Clarence Holliday was a 15-year-old musician. The couple soon parted, and Billie was brought up by her grandparents. In her teens a neighbour tried to rape her and she was sent to a Catholic home for wayward girls. But her grandparents engineered her release and she went to New York to join her mother, who was working as a maid.

Billie got a job as a maid but began frequenting nightclubs and jazz haunts and dabbling in prostitution. After spending four months in a welfare institution she went back to the clubs, this time earning money by singing. At 22 she joined Count Basie and his band but had a row and was fired after a year. Then she joined bandleader Artie Shaw.

Being the only black singer with a white band made her a controversial figure, and there were racial incidents in the South. She finally left Artie after a New York hotel where the band was to play made her use the back door and told her not to mix with the guests.

Billie — who had taken the name in her teens from her movie idol Billie Dove — suffered dreadfully from stage fright, which she overcame at first with drink and marijuana. In the forties, during a brief, unhappy marriage to club owner Jimmy Monroe, she found a new companion in heroin. Soon nearly all her money was going to feed her addiction, and her career was suffering.

On the advice of her manager she went into an expensive New York clinic to be cured and, ironically, it was this that attracted the attention of the police. The Narcotics Squad began trailing her and eventually arrested her for possessing drugs. She served nine months in jail and came out cured of her drug habit — for a while.

The rest of Billie's life was punctuated by returns to drug-taking, more cures and more arrests. Each time she came off heroin she turned to gin with greater vengeance, and her health was cracking up. In 1959 she collapsed after two numbers at a Greenwich Village concert and went into hospital with cardiac failure and liver problems.

Scandal followed her. Police searched her hospital room and claimed to have found a packet of heroin. She was again charged with possession and, technically under arrest, her flowers, magazines and most personal possessions were confiscated. She died on 17 July at the age of 44, with just 750 dollars and 70 cents to her name.

When John Lennon was shot dead by a crazed gunman outside his New York home it was a senseless and unfitting end for the man who had spent more than ten years campaigning for peace and preaching brotherly love. But in life Lennon was very far from the saintly image he bequeathed to the world.

He loved to scandalize, and his talent for making shock headlines came through even after his death. A TV tribute to him shown in America included scenes of him and Yoko making love. The eight-minute clip, which showed the couple naked in bed kissing and caressing each other, was recorded at their New York flat shortly before he was killed. Many fans were upset that his widow Yoko Ono saw fit to release the film to promote her single *Walking On Thin Ice*.

In the Beatles' early days in Hamburg and Liverpool, Lennon was brash and loud-mouthed, with greasy hairstyle and old black leathers, and he gave full rein to his urge to shock. At Hamburg's Star Club he would walk on stage naked except for a lavatory seat round his neck. On Sundays he would stand on a balcony and taunt passing churchgoers. He once tied a water-filled contraceptive sheath to a figure of Christ and put it out for churchgoers to see. Another time he urinated over the heads of three nuns. After the Beatles received their MBEs in 1965 he claimed that he and the others had smoked marijuana in the toilets at Buckingham Palace.

As Beatlemania took the world by storm John was experimenting with heroin and cocaine as well as smoking pot. In 1964 he began a crazy four-year drugs binge that almost killed him. 'I went on LSD and must have had a thousand trips,' he said. His introduction to LSD came in the mid-sixties at the home of a friend, a dentist, who spiked his guests' coffee with the drug.

Cynthia, his first wife, who was with him, said: 'It was terrifying. We finally came out of it eight hours later, back at George Harrison's place. I made up my mind never to repeat the experience. But John thought it was wonderful. I couldn't pull him back. There were all

The Beatles, 1967

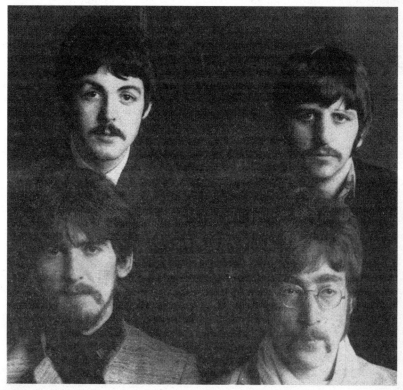

those people around him saying, "I can invent an island where there is sunshine all the time," and John believed them.

'The Beatles thought drugs would somehow improve their lives. But it didn't work. John needed to escape from reality. He wanted to experience more than the life he was leading offered. As far as I was concerned the rot set in the moment cannabis and LSD seeped into our lives. Life became a nightmare.'

Millions were shocked by allegations that Lennon had an affair with Beatles' manager Brian Epstein, a known homosexual who died in 1966. In his book *You Don't Have To Say You Love Me* record producer Simon Napier-Bell recalled Epstein talking about 'the first time I got to kiss John after I'd been crazy about him for ages'.

Commenting on his claim, Napier-Bell said: 'Epstein implied he had been to bed with John without ever saying so.' He added that Lennon's interest was short-lived. Lennon himself, a few weeks before he died, said he came close to having an affair with Epstein. 'It was almost an affair but not quite,' he said. 'It was never consummated.'

In contrast with Lennon, his one-time song-writing partner Paul McCartney appears almost angelic. But many have been shocked by his oft-aired view, in a world gripped by a massive drugs problem, that cannabis should be legalized and his admission that he smoked it regularly.

Like the other Beatles, he experimented with hard drugs in the sixties but soon saw the danger and stuck to cannabis ever since. He has said: 'Though hard drugs are bad and dangerous, soft drugs are less toxic than alcohol. Make it like consenting adults in private. If they want to do it, let them.'

McCartney has been in regular trouble with the law over drugs. In 1972 he, his wife Linda and a member of the Wings group were fined a total of £800 in Sweden for possessing cannabis. Later that year McCartney was fined £100 following a raid on his farmhouse home at Campbeltown, Scotland, in which five cannabis plants were found.

In 1980 he was detained in a Tokyo police cell for more than a week accused of trying to smuggle half a pound of cannabis into Japan as he flew in for a Wings concert tour. He was never charged, but ordered to leave the country. Cancellation of the tour cost him an estimated £700,000 — nearly £100,000 per ounce of cannabis.

In 1984 he and Linda were fined £70 each by a Barbados court after marijuana was seized at their holiday home. Less than two weeks later Linda was fined £75 by a West London court when she admitted smuggling cannabis into Britain. Defiantly she called the conviction 'much ado about nothing'.

A friend said: 'Linda loves to give two fingers to the Establishment. It's her way of getting thrills.' Which is more or less the story of rock'n' roll.

Elvis Presley

Elvis Presley was the king of rock who could not cope with his 'royal' status. The fame, the fan worship, the ready availability of unlimited girls, drugs and whatever else he craved were too much for him to handle. He wanted it all . . . and it killed him.

Above all, it was the drugs that wrought his destruction. Everyone close to Presley was worried by his drugtaking. Not marijuana, heroin or cocaine, though he had tried them all. The King was hooked on pills — on tranquillizers, anti-depressants and sleeping tablets. He used drugs to control his every physical and mental function. He took them to go to sleep, to wake up, to go to the lavatory. Sometimes he would be so high on amphetamines — 'uppers' — that he could hardly breathe.

He took Quaaludes, known in Hollywood as the 'love drug' because they heighten sexual pleasure, in the hope that they would restore his waning performance.

The astonishing story of how the idolized rock king fell from grace and finally became an obese, pain-racked, erratic, shambling, drug-degraded zombie is graphically revealed in two remarkable books. The first — *Elvis: What Happened* (Ballantine Books) — was compiled by ace New York newsman Steve Dunleavy. It tells the story of Presley's astonishing lifestyle through the mouths of three of his ex-aides: Red West, his brother Sonny and Dave Hebler. The second book is by Presley's stepmother and her three sons, following his father's remarriage. In *Elvis We Love You Tender* (Delacorte Press) Dee Presley and her boys Billy, Rick and David Stanley reveal: 'Elvis was on sleeping pills, pep pills, morphine and Demerol virtually all the time.'

According to David Stanley, Presley would issue orders to his aides as soon as they arrived in a new town, urging them to track down doctors who would prescribe the huge daily doses of pills he needed. Once, in Las Vegas, the aides failed him. Stepbrother David Stanley recalled: 'He jumped on a table, pulled out his gun and said, "I'll buy a goddam drug store if I want to. I'm going to get what I want. You people had better realize that either you're with me or you're against me." '

Presley's personal doctor, Dr George Nichopoulos, was suspended from medical practice for three months after being found guilty of over-prescribing drugs to the singer and nine other people. He was also placed on probation for three years by the Tennessee State Board of Medical Examiners.

But according to Presley's aides, most of his drugs came from outside sources. A former bodyguard said: 'Other doctors prescribed far more drugs than Dr Nichopoulos. There was one in Memphis who was handy with the prescription pad. And there was also a very obliging specialist in Memphis. Elvis had a doctor in Las Vegas to keep him supplied, plus two in Palm Springs and two in Beverly Hills. And when he was on tour, he would just call a local doctor wherever he was and get whatever he wanted.'

Presley used to reward his doctors with very expensive gifts such as Cadillacs, after which they felt obliged to prescribe whatever he asked for. And they enjoyed the enormous prestige of being one of Elvis Presley's doctors.

Former bodyguard Dave Hebler said: 'No one forced the pills down Elvis's throat. It was the other way round. There was no conspiracy to get Elvis to become a junkie. He was far from an unwilling victim. He demanded drugs and he used pressure to get them.'

Elvis got into drugs in the sixties when he was making three films a year, driving cross-country for 24 hours at a stretch, going on dates, having parties and playing marathon football games. He ran a football club called Elvis Presley Enterprises. Everyone in the team would be asked to swallow two uppers. They could then play four or five games straight off, according to ex-bodyguard Red West. After the uppers came painkillers for football injuries and, slowly, the rock king became a walking chemist's shop.

When, in the seventies, he resumed touring, he needed the amphetamines more than ever to help him call on his last reserves of energy. And when he began to put on weight, he took more uppers to suppress his appetite. Ever-larger doses were needed for the same effect. Eventually he reached the point where his drugtaking was completely out of hand.

Rick Stanley said: 'He didn't show moderation. Not just with drugs, but with anything he did. There were no half measures. In 1972–3 he started getting into needles. That's when I really started to worry, when he became a needle head. His body began to look like a pin cushion. In his last year he just didn't care any more. He'd fall asleep in the middle of eating and nearly choke to death.'

He was regularly taken into hospital, needing treatment for an enlarged colon and a liver infection, and for futile attempts to get him off drugs. The trouble was that there were always plenty of people prepared to smuggle the drugs in to him.

His concerts were often disasters. Sometimes he had to read the words of his hits from prompt boards held by stage hands or from a song sheet he'd pull from his pocket. Or he would ramble incoherently to the audience for half an hour while they waited for a song. At Las Vegas he once spent 28 minutes on stage giving a karate demonstration. Hundreds walked out.

Elvis Presley

After one concert in Baltimore, a theatre spokesman said: 'It was a shambles. He was so ill I don't think he knew where he was. It was a struggle for him to sing his songs. He seemed to have forgotten most of the words. At one stage he dropped his mike and a bodyguard came on stage with another, which he held while Presley played his guitar for 20 minutes. The fans began booing because they wanted to hear him sing, not play.

'Eventually he collapsed and was carried into his dressing room. His bodyguards allowed no one in but his doctor with his medical bag. Thirty minutes later Presley reappeared looking refreshed, went back on stage and sang four or five more songs. He forgot a lot of the words and when he tried to apologize he couldn't put a sentence together.'

As the drugs took their toll of his body, the idol who had been a sex symbol for a generation of adolescent girls was becoming almost impotent. He did, however, have his memories. Shortly before he married his beautiful wife Priscilla, he told his stepmother Dee that he had taken a thousand women to bed. There were many more to follow.

His stepbrother Billy said: 'Wherever he went there were girls waiting to do his bidding. They'd crate themselves in boxes, go to bed with roadies, do anything just to get near him. He had more girls than anybody. Sometimes we'd round them up like cattle and take them to his room for him to look over. If none of them took his fancy he'd tell us to keep them on ice — keep them nearby in case he changed his mind.'

One of these auditions for the role of Presley's bedmate was described by Ellen Polton, a girl who was invited to meet him in California. She said: 'Elvis was sitting at the centre of a horseshoe-shaped couch, feet up on a coffee table, captain's hat on his head, with half a dozen girls sitting on the couch on each side of him.' After looking the girls over Presley would smile at the winner. The rest had to put up with being his pals' perks for the night.

Red West supported Presley's early reputation as a superstud. He said: 'Once he realized how easily he could get girls we were routing them through his bedroom two and sometimes three a day.'

When the Memphis Mafia — as Presley's team of bodyguards and henchmen became known — were selecting girls for the boss they had to remember that he liked them petite and feminine, with small feet.

He had varied sexual inclinations, and indulged them all. At Grace-land, his Memphis home, he had two-way mirrors fitted through which he could watch girls undressing to go swimming. In another part of the house he and the boys could watch couples make love in a bedroom. And he liked to record his own performances with a video camera in his bedroom.

Once he wanted to try wife-swapping. He shocked bodyguard Sonny

West by suggesting it when they were on a plane with their wives, Priscilla and Judy. West recalled: 'He said he knew I liked Priscilla, and he liked Judy, so why didn't we swap for a bit of fun. The girls were terribly embarrassed and so was I. I treated it as if he was joking and, thank God, the conversation moved on to something else.'

On one terrifying occasion Presley almost killed himself and the girl fan with drugs. The girl, Page Peterson, was a beautiful 18-year-old blonde when she met the King in 1971. A devoted Presley fan, she went to a Las Vegas concert with her mother. As she watched her idol strut, pout and flick his hips on stage she thought she would gladly die in his arms. And she nearly did.

Presley soon spotted the knockout beauty in the second row. As he swung into his last number, *I Can't Help Falling In Love With You,* he could not take his eyes off her. When he came off stage he told a bodyguard there was 'a beautiful piece of woman' sitting near the front. His aide knew exactly what to do.

Page said later: 'A couple of minutes after the curtain came down, when everyone was still screaming and cheering, one of Elvis's helpers came up to me and asked if I wanted to meet Elvis. I went to meet him in his dressing room and he talked to me about God and politics. He asked me to stay, but I said my mother and I were going to sleep in our car. He insisted on getting us a hotel room, but I stayed with Elvis in his room. I went to Las Vegas again with him after that, and later I stayed with him for two weeks.'

When Page visited him in Palm Springs, California, she complained of a terrible headache. 'He gave me something, I think it was pills,' she said. 'I don't remember anything else until I woke up in hospital.'

During Page's lost hours, Presley was feeding both of them a whole range of drugs. Sonny West told of sounds of giggling, stumbling and slurred words coming from the master bedroom at 4 a.m. Presley's aides found the couple unconscious in the bedroom the following afternoon. They were naked and barely breathing. A doctor and ambulance were called and the critically ill pair had their stomachs pumped out in hospital.

'I remember the doctor being angry at all the drugs that were in me,' Page said. 'Elvis called my mother and a plane was sent to pick her up. I was in intensive care for two weeks. Later Elvis told me he had paid 10,000 dollars in bribes so the whole thing could be hushed up. But I didn't have any bad feelings towards him. He didn't come to see me because he would have been recognized. He sent me a verse from the Bible, though. And he paid all the bills.'

In his last, sad years of decline he was going for girls much younger than himself. Some were half his age. New York psychologist Dr William van Precht said: 'He had a weight problem which would have made him unsure of his sex appeal, and he linked sex appeal with success. Relationships with younger women kept him feeling young and helped him forget he was growing older.' To their disappointment, the dates were often purely platonic, because of his fear of failure.

In the end nothing could halt the pace of his self-destruction. He was on a roller-coaster to oblivion.

Some time before 2.30 in the afternoon of 16 August 1977, alone in his bathroom and wearing a pair of blue cotton pyjamas, Presley dropped the book he had been reading and keeled over on his face. As he gasped desperately for breath, his heart gave out. The 'king' was dead.

Ginger Alden, Presley's last girlfriend, who was with him immediately before he died, said she had tried to stop him taking drugs. He refused, saying: 'I need them.' She saw him take a vast number of pills the night before she found him dead in his bathroom. An analysis of his blood found ten different drugs in his body, including codeine, morphine and Quaalude. Their interaction had caused heart failure.

Tennessee public health investigator Steve Belsky said: 'Elvis Presley, from my experience, was issued more scheduled uppers, downers and amphetamines than any other individual I have ever seen.'

Los Angeles drugs expert Jack Kelly, now a private detective, said Presley was the victim of unscrupulous doctors. He said: 'Some doctors get their patients addicted through carelessness, some for profit, and some because they're star struck. Elvis was a victim of all three.'

Fatty Arbuckle

Twenty-stone Fatty Arbuckle was one of the most successful comedians in the world. His only serious screen rival at the height of his fame was Charlie Chaplin. Yet after one party at a San Francisco hotel in 1921 his career was in ruins. He was disgraced, vilified, effectively run out of Hollywood and was never again able to work under his own name.

The party, with about 50 guests, began at the St Francis Hotel on the night of Friday, 2 September. It went on through Saturday and Sunday and Monday.

At mid-morning on Monday, as most of the revellers lay in a drunken stupor, actors' agent Al Semnacher arrived with four pretty young starlets. The party roared back to life.

Arbuckle, dancing with a starlet, accidentally spilled wine on her dress. She did a striptease to the music and carried on dancing.

Another starlet, Virginia Rappe, was getting hopelessly drunk. She stumbled to the bathroom adjoining Arbuckle's room. Shortly afterwards the star went into his own bedroom. The party went on.

Later squeals — or screams — were heard from the bedroom. When guests knocked on the door it was opened by Arbuckle. Virginia was lying on the bed moaning. She was assumed to be drunk, and when she later became hysterical she was dumped in a cold bath to calm her down. Then she was put in another bedroom to sleep off the effects of the drink.

The wild party went on until the early hours of Tuesday. By then, according to one of the starlets, most of the guests were naked and there was 'open copulation'. At last they fell into a mass, drunken slumber.

On Wednesday morning Virginia was still in bed, still moaning and looking very ill. A doctor was called. He diagnosed alcoholic poisoning and called an ambulance.

Two days later Virginia died in hospital. A doctor gave peritonitis as the cause. But when a post-mortem was carried out it was discovered that the girl had a ruptured bladder and superficial bruising to the body.

Virginia's friends accused Arbuckle of rape and murder. The comedian was arrested. The charge of murder was later reduced to manslaughter.

American filmgoers were horrified. Their fat, jolly idol who wouldn't harm a fly was being held up as a killer, rapist, pervert and drunkard. Cinema screens were pelted when his films appeared. The boss of Arbuckle's Hollywood studios tried to intercede with the San Francisco district attorney, and was immediately warned that he could himself face charges of bribery and attempting to pervert the course of justice.

The star, tried under his real name of Roscoe Arbuckle, was found not guilty, but the district attorney was dissatisfied and ordered a retrial. Again the jury acquitted him, saying that 'a grave injustice has been done him'. Arbuckle celebrated — but not for long.

A 'clean-up Hollywood' committee was set up by the studios and Arbuckle was banned from working for eight months. In fact he was never able to work again under his own name. His producer Mack Sennett had the studios fumigated. Paramount buried new, unshown films previously made by the comic. Actors were made to sign contractual clauses promising to behave decently. Censorship was introduced, and a strict code of morality for films was laid down.

In 1933 a totally destroyed Fatty Arbuckle was offered his first full acting role in 12 years. He readily accepted. The next day he fell dead of a heart attack.

Charlie Chaplin

The life and career of Fatty Arbuckle were totally destroyed by one sensational court case. And the same fate almost befell his principal comic rival, Charlie Chaplin, when a paternity suit was slapped on him by an angry young starlet in 1943.

Chaplin, then 53, was almost three times the age of the girl, Joan Barry, when he signed her up on a $75-a-week contract, gave her acting lessons and had her teeth fixed. The thrice-wed Chaplin made love to Joan at his Los Angeles home and spent some time with her in New York.

The affair lasted two years before Chaplin tired of her, but Joan continued to pester him. She took an overdose but failed to rekindle his interest. She called at his home and threatened him. Eventually Chaplin had her arrested and thrown into police cells. She was sentenced to a month's jail, but the decision was immediately reversed when a prison doctor discovered she was pregnant.

In June 1943 she brought a paternity suit against Chaplin. Federal authorities compounded the charge by accusing the star of transporting a girl across state lines for immoral purposes. The use of this anti-prostitution law was rejected after proceedings in which Chaplin openly wept in court.

But at the ensuing paternity case Chaplin received a rougher ride. Joan's lawyers branded the comic as 'a master mechanic in the art of seduction'. Joan, who took her baby to court every day, described some of their romantic romps.

The defence argued that Joan was only after Chaplin's money and had had other lovers while seeing the star. Blood tests appeared to prove that Chaplin was not the father, but despite the weight of evidence, the comedian was ordered to make a settlement on the child.

Until his death, on Christmas Day 1977 at the age of 88, Chaplin believed that the verdict had gone against him because of public and media bias over his 'left-wing' views. He later left the country to live abroad. However, revelations which followed his death showed that his passion for the young Joan Barry had not been an isolated affair.

According to his second wife Lita Grey, Chaplin had a sordid interest in young girls. She said he was sexually fascinated by them, and that he had seduced her when she was 15.

In her book *My Life With Chaplin* she wrote: 'He liked to cultivate them, to gain their trust, to be their first — never their second — lover. He believed that the most beautiful form of life was a very young girl just starting to bloom.'

He once told Lita: 'Some Mr Novembers can be disgusting when they're with some Miss Mays, eager to corrupt innocence. I'm not like that — God knows that I'm not.'

Lita's book told of his seduction attempts after he had agreed to give her a screen test for the female lead in *The Gold Rush*. He put his hand up her skirt in the back of his car, curtained from the chauffeur's view. Her yell of fear stopped him going further. Eventually Chaplin succeeded into seducing Lita in his Hollywood mansion. After that, she said, they could not keep their hands off one another.

When Lita became pregnant he tried to talk her into having an abortion. She refused. So he offered her $20,000 to marry someone else. Again she refused. It was only at the insistence of Lita's mother that he finally agreed to marry her. They wed when she was 16 and he was 35.

Lita said her husband always refused to use contraceptives, and when she again became pregnant — and again rejected his demand that she have an abortion — he became furious.

He shouted: 'You've ruined me. You forced me to marry you with one baby and now you're trying to ruin me completely with another one. I don't want it. I don't want you. I don't want anything except to be left alone to do my work.'

Their marriage lasted three years. Chaplin made a generous settlement on Lita and their children after an amazing threat by her . . . that she would reveal to the world the names of the five famous women she said he had made love to during their marriage.

Chaplin finally found lasting happiness with Oona O'Neill, his fourth wife. They wed and had their first child during the Joan Barry paternity scandal. He was 54 and she was 18.

Fiona Richmond

British writer and actress Fiona Richmond appeared naked in magazines, on stage and in films. She made her name in the 1970s writing highly detailed accounts of her bedroom antics in a magazine, and she was star attraction at a nightclub where she swam naked in a large transparent tank. She once told a reporter: 'I don't believe in wasting time with a man. If I want to go to bed with him I go straight up to him and tell him. It does away with all the boring preliminaries. After all, every girl nowadays knows that when she is wined and dined all the man wants is breakfast in bed.'

Extraordinarily, Fiona's father was a country vicar and her mother a schoolmistress. But even more oddly, they both expressed themselves delighted with their daughter's sexy successes. 'I'm tickled pink,' her mother said. Fiona found a husband who was equally understanding. She gave up her erotic career and settled down and married in 1982.

Marilyn Monroe

Just before dawn on Sunday, 5 August 1962 the naked body of Marilyn Monroe was discovered sprawled across her bed.

The greatest sex goddess of all had been married four times and had countless lovers. Yet she died alone. And in death, as in life, she was surrounded by mystery, innuendo and scandal.

The years that have passed since her death have not dimmed her legend. Instead it has been fanned by revelations of her amazing sexual exploits, outrageous behaviour and secret affairs with stars and politicians — including, it is alleged, US President Jack Kennedy himself.

It has been revealed that she had a baby when she was 15, that she became a bar prostitute, that she performed sexual favours for studio tycoons and that she ended up seeking gratification with her masseur and her chauffeur.

Ironically, the sex goddess lusted after by millions often failed to find satisfaction in sex. In her frenzied affairs she was seeking a joy and a release that seldom came to her. She once said she was hooked on sex like an alcoholic is hooked on liquor. And there were plenty of opportunities to indulge her craving. 'My body turns people on like an electric light,' she said.

The girl the world came to know as Marilyn Monroe was born Norma Jean Mortenson on 1 June 1926 in Los Angeles.

Her mother Gladys, a film cutter, was emotionally disturbed.

Marilyn never knew for sure who her father was. He may have been Edward Mortenson, a Danish baker later killed in a motorcycle accident. Or he could have been C. Stanley Gifford, her mother's boss.

Just 12 days after her birth her mother was carted off to an asylum after trying to slit a friend's throat. Marilyn was to spend the next 15 years in children's homes and with a succession of foster parents. Shuttled from home to home, she became a shy, nervous girl who panicked easily.

Tragedy struck early. At 15 she was seduced by one of her foster fathers. She went to live with her Aunt Grace, and found she was pregnant. She was overjoyed with her baby boy, but her aunt insisted on having him adopted.

'It was like being kicked in the head,' Marilyn said. 'I begged them not to take my baby away, but they said it was the best thing.

'They said I was too young to take care of him. They took him from me and I never saw him again.'

She was pushed into her first marriage, to boy-next-door Jim Dougherty, by her Aunt Grace, who wanted her off her hands.

The life of a working-class housewife soon bored her, and escape came when Dougherty was called up in World War II. They lived for a while on a base in California where she killed time in bars.

She soon discovered she could make money by going to men's hotel rooms with them.

Years later, telling her maid Lena Pepitone of those escapades, she said: 'I let my husband Jim do whatever he wanted with me even though I didn't really love him. So what was the difference?'

After Jim was posted abroad she built up her new career until she met an agent who advised her to use her powers of seduction to become a movie star.

A natural brunette, she decided early on that gentlemen prefer blondes. But she went further than her famous bleached hairstyle.

She also peroxided her pubic hair — a painful process but essential with her habit of wearing sheer white dresses and no underwear.

As a model, she began getting invited to Hollywood parties. There she met the big studio moguls and distributed her favours freely.

There was the Twentieth-Century Fox founder Joe Schenk, who was 70 and asked only that she sat with him in the nude while he fondled her breasts and talked about the good old days.

And Columbia boss Harry Cohn who, she said, simply told her to get into bed.

In her fight for a toehold on the ladder to stardom, she admitted later that she would have slept with almost anybody, so long as they were 'nice'.

She told Lena: 'If I made them happy, why not? It didn't hurt. I like to see men smile.'

It was the film *Asphalt Jungle* that put her on the map. Suddenly she was the star of the cocktail parties, the luscious ripe peach of a girl with a walk that spoke volumes. Being blonde and deliciously beautiful, she was slotted into the dumb blonde category.

Producer Billy Wilder said: 'She has breasts like granite and a brain like cheese.'

In fact she was far from dumb, and craved intelligent conversation.

She may even have sought an affair with Einstein, the great mathematician. She once confessed to actress Shelley Winters that she fancied him. Shelley told her there was no chance — he was the most famous scientist of the century, and an old man besides.

Marilyn replied: 'That has nothing to do with it. Anyway, I hear he's very young for his age.'

After her death a large framed photograph of Einstein was found among her possessions. On it was written: 'To Marilyn, with love and thanks, Albert Einstein.'

As a model, Marilyn had no qualms about posing nude, but friends dismiss stories that she starred in pornographic films.

Her famous calendar shot, lying naked on red velvet, was tame by today's standards, but studio bosses were horrified and ordered her to deny having posed for it.

She refused, and told everyone she had done it to pay the rent.

Third husband Joe di Maggio hated her sex goddess image. He reckoned the only place she should be sexy was at home with him. He would do nothing to help her career, refusing to pose for publicity shots with her, and never accompanying her to showbiz parties.

They parted after nine months.

'What good is being a sex symbol if it drives your man away?' she said bitterly.

But even before she married di Maggio, she was carrying a torch for playwright Arthur Miller.

When she married him she felt she had proved an important point. She was not just a dumb blonde. She was the wife of an intellectual.

'I've never loved anyone as much as I love Arthur,' she said.

But her happiness was short-lived.

She longed for a child by Miller, and soon became pregnant. But she had a miscarriage after the sixth week.

When her next pregnancy ended the same way she was beside herself with grief, sobbing: 'I can never have kids again.'

Miller was soon spending little time with his beautiful wife. He shut himself away in his study working all day and late into the evening.

Sometimes, after Marilyn had pleaded to be taken out to dinner or to a show, he would half-promise to do so — as soon as he had finished his work.

In a flurry of excitement she would dress and make up, then wait for him, looking her most stunning, but nearly always Miller would finally call off the date, claiming to be too busy.

Sobbing with rage and disappointment, Marilyn would rip off her clothes and go to bed alone.

As she and Miller drifted further apart she turned to champagne, pills and a succession of affairs with all kinds of men, from politicians to a plumber working in her apartment block.

She fell for French star Yves Montand as soon as she met him, and fought to have him as her co-star in *Let's Make Love*. She won.

A brief affair flourished during filming, when Arthur Miller was away in Ireland and Montand's wife Simone Signoret had gone back to Paris. As so often happened with the men in her life, Marilyn hoped their affair would lead to marriage.

But, filming over, Montand thanked her for a 'nice time' and flew straight back to his wife. Marilyn was left sobbing among the flowers and unopened champagne bottles in a hotel room she had booked for a romantic farewell.

The end of her marriage to Miller came during filming of *The Misfits*,

Marilyn Monroe with playwright Arthur Miller

which he wrote. Her blazing rows with him on set were blamed for the death of co-star Clark Gable a day after filming ended.

Miller left her at the same time.

With her marriage in ruins, and certain that she was partly to blame for Gable's death, she turned back to Joe di Maggio for consolation.

And when he wasn't around, it was booze, pills and a succession of lovers. Any available man was fair game for the insatiable love goddess.

She hired a tall, handsome masseur, and seduced him at their afternoon sessions.

Other days she would invite her chauffeur to her room, and lock the door for several hours.

She had a passionate affair with young screenwriter Hans Lembourne, who later became a Danish MP.

She told him: 'I don't know whether I'm good or bad in bed. I can't sustain loving relationships.

'I drink, I lie. I often want to die — though I'm deadly scared of death.

'I believe in marriage and faithfulness, yet I go to bed with others when I'm married. God help me, what a mess.'

Marilyn was terrified of ending her days in an asylum, like her mother and grandparents.

She told Lembourne: 'I resemble my mother. I'm afraid I'll go mad like her.'

Her maid Lena Pepitone was stunned when she first met Marilyn for her interview. The famous star was totally nude, as she usually was around the house.

In her book *Marilyn Monroe Confidential*, Lena said:

'Her blonde hair looked unwashed, and was a mess.

I was astonished by the way she smelled. She needed a bath, badly. Without make-up she was pale and tired-looking. Her celebrated figure seemed more overweight than voluptuous.

As she sprawled on a white couch she brought to mind a de luxe prostitute after a busy night in a plush brothel.

Lena grew fond of her unpredictable boss, but she was horrified by some of her sluttish ways.

She recalls how the star would gnaw the meat off a bone, then drop it on the bedclothes, wiping her greasy hands on the sheets.

Marilyn craved affection in any form — be it sex, praise, or adulation from her fans. Deprived of it, she would sink into a black depression, drinking champagne and Bloody Marys and swallowing pills by the handful.

She said: 'I've slept with too many men. But at least I loved them all.

'I drink more than I should, and I take so many pills that they could kill me. But I can't sleep.'

She genuinely hoped that a friendship with Frank Sinatra would lead to marriage, but he insisted she keep out of sight when she was staying at his place.

He was having affairs with other women, and did not want any publicity.

One evening, drunk on champagne and tired of waiting for him, she wandered nude into the room where Sinatra and his friends had a poker school going.

Furious, he hissed: 'Get your fat ass upstairs!'

Sinatra did not propose, and she was heartbroken when she heard he was dating leggy dancer Juliet Prowse.

It was, she was convinced, Juliet's legs that gave her the edge, and she became aware that her own legs were not her best feature.

Leg-improvement exercises became the order of the day.

Marilyn's sensational sexuality and her craving for love took her to the very top — to President John Kennedy, who used to pinch and squeeze her and tell her dirty jokes.

He was fond of putting his hand up her skirt at the dinner table. One night he kept going until he discovered she wasn't wearing panties.

He took his hand away fast!

'He hadn't counted on going that far,' Marilyn said.

In the last year of her life the sex goddess was noticing the signs of age . . . and she hated them.

She said her breasts were getting flabby, and she worried about stretch marks on her bust and bottom.

'I can't act,' she told Lena. 'When my face and body go I'll be finished.'

She even stuttered, an affliction the cause of which dated back to her childhood. She told a friend: 'When I was nine a man forced me to do something. I've never got over it and now I stutter when I'm angry or upset.'

Marilyn's last picture was called *Something's Got To Give* — and something did.

Taking more pills than ever, she often did not arrive on the set until the afternoon. Sometimes she did not turn up at all. She was fired. Her co-star Dean Martin quit. The film was abandoned.

Two months later, on the morning of 5 August 1962, Marilyn was found dead in bed, at her newly acquired home on Fifth Helena Drive in Brentwood, Los Angeles. Tell-tale empty pill bottles were on the bedside table.

The conclusion was obvious . . . Marilyn had committed suicide. The inquest verdict went unquestioned for some months. But when at last doubts were raised, the resultant scandal threatened to be bigger than anything the actress had created in her lifetime.

For the question more and more people began to ask was: Who killed Marilyn Monroe? Did she die by her own hand — by accident or suicide — or was she murdered?

When her body was found she had been clutching a telephone. Who had she been trying to ring?

Soon rumours of her supposed affairs with both Jack Kennedy and his brother Robert, the attorney-general, were common currency. According to one of her closest friends, Robert Slatzer, Marilyn had two important meetings planned for the day following her death. One was with her lawyer, the other was a press conference.

At this conference, said Slatzer, Marilyn planned to reveal the truth about her relationship with Jack Kennedy or Robert Kennedy, or possibly both. She felt that the Kennedys had used her, then abandoned her — her calls to the White House were no longer being accepted — and she was out for revenge. The only thing that would stop her revelations, she had said, would have been a phone call from or a meeting with Robert Kennedy on the night of 4 August.

That night Marilyn was due to have attended a dinner at the home of Peter Lawford and his wife Pat, sister of the Kennedy brothers. The actress had met Robert Kennedy at the house on several occasions. Robert Kennedy may have been planning to turn up. He never did.

Nor did Marilyn, who at about 8 p.m. received a phone call from Peter Lawford asking if she was on her way. According to Lawford's testimony, she said she felt too tired. She told him:

'Say goodbye to Pat and say goodbye to the president — and say goodbye to yourself, because you're such a nice guy!'

There were rumours at the time that Robert Kennedy, staying at the St Francis Hotel, San Francisco, had travelled south to Los Angeles on the night of 4 August for a meeting with Monroe. The rumours were strongly denied.

Christa Helm

Beautiful blonde starlet Christa Helm, a 27-year-old *Playboy* bunnygirl, was stabbed to death in 1977 — possibly because of the sensational love diary she kept.

Christa had arrived in Hollywood dreaming of stardom. When the dream failed to materialize and her money ran out she became one of the movie capital's hundreds of good-time girls. She was a familiar face at showbusiness parties, and she boasted of affairs with a dozen top film and pop stars.

A former boyfriend, film director Ron Walsh, said: 'I know some of the men she had affairs with and they're people who certainly wouldn't want that to be known. She was proud of her lifestyle and the celebrities she knew intimately. Her diary had a lot of names and embarrassing details.'

Christa had announced plans to write a book that would 'lift the lid off Hollywood's love life'. She never got the chance.

She was stabbed to death in the street as she left one party and was on the way to another. Police found her with her car ignition key still clutched in her hand. She had 20 knife wounds in her body.

Detective William Tiner of the West Hollywood homicide squad said: 'It is very possible that she was killed by someone she knew because of what she knew.'

Her diary has never been found.

Rudolf Valentino

Rudolph Valentino's screen image was as 'the great lover'. In his private life, however, he failed to live up to this virile reputation. His first wife locked him out of the bedroom on his wedding night. The second made him act like a servant and call her 'boss'. Both women had lesbian tendencies, and neither marriage was consummated. Valentino, a vet's son from southern Italy, whose two passions were good food and young men, became distraught when the American press taunted him for using powder make-up. On his deathbed at a New York hospital where he was being treated for peritonitis in 1926 he asked his doctor: 'Do I really act like a pink powder puff?'

Another sensational theory was that the FBI had been involved in the star's death. FBI chief J. Edgar Hoover's agents collected for him every scrap of information about the private lives of leading politicians. It was one of the reasons Hoover's eccentric handling of the FBI had previously gone unchallenged. And in the Kennedys' case, the FBI's personal files bulged with scandal.

Neither John nor his younger brother had been suitably secretive in their extra-marital activities. In the case of Marilyn Monroe, it was thought that her state of depression and suspected nervous disorder might indeed cause her to spill the beans.

Marilyn's telephone was believed to have been bugged — possibly by the FBI — and it has been suggested by more than one investigator that it was the federal law enforcement agency that was given the task of silencing her.

A bizarre twist to this theory was made in 1981 by a reformed criminal, Ronald 'Sonny' Gibson. In a book *Mafia Kingpin* Gibson said that while working for the Mob he had been told that Marilyn had been murdered by Mafia hitmen. J. Edgar Hoover, he said, had been furious about the actress's affairs with top politicians, so the Mafia had taken upon themselves the task of silencing her as a means of repaying favours done them by the FBI.

Certainly Gibson is not alone in his assertion that Marilyn died not because she had swallowed an overdose of barbiturates but because drugs had been injected into her. Even top pathologists who investigated the case have since gone into print to say the same.

Officially the overdose that killed the star was more than 50 sleeping tablets. Marilyn, according to her aides, had great difficulty swallowing tablets without large quantities of water. Police who were called to the house in Fifth Helena Drive found no glass in the bedroom. A post-mortem showed virtually no fluid in her stomach. And, strangely, there was little trace of the drug in the victim's digestive tract — all evidence that points to an intruder injecting the deadly barbiturate dose directly into her body.

As retired Los Angeles police sergeant Jack Clemmons, the first officer to arrive on the scene, said: 'I was shocked to high heaven by the official verdict of suicide.

'It was obviously a case of murder.'

But by whom? The answer, if the theory were ever proved, would create the scandal of the century.

Lana Turner

Lana Turner was the original 'sweater girl'. Her film career had begun while she was still a schoolgirl. A series of hit movies followed — then a string of flops. Which is how her four failed marriages and several love affairs could also have been described.

In 1957 her muddled marital arrangements and her shaky career seemed to have turned the corner. She was 37, living with her teenaged daughter from her second marriage — and she had a major hit on her hands. Her new movie *Peyton Place* was a nationwide box-office sellout. She had even been nominated for an Oscar.

Then a fresh disaster walked into her life. She received a phone call from a total stranger who mentioned the names of some supposed mutual friends and asked her out on a blind date. Extraordinarily, she agreed. The smooth-talking stranger was Johnny Stompanato, an ex-US Marine, con-man and associate of known gangsters. They became lovers, and the film star allowed the seedy crook to move into her Los Angeles mansion. There he bullied her, abused her, took her money and spent it on gambling. They fought interminably, but Lana Turner appeared not to be able to live without him.

On the night of 4 April 1958 Stompanato had a screaming row with his mistress. He threatened to scar her at the very least. Listening outside the door was Lana's 14-year-old daughter Cheryl. She entered the room carrying a long-bladed kitchen knife, thrust it into his stomach and killed him.

The ensuing inquest was sensational. Televised live, it got audience figures higher even than *Peyton Place*. And the story revealed in it was racier than any movie.

Even the couple's love letters were produced as every detail of the sordid affair was aired. Lana Turner gave the performance of her life in the witness box. Her daughter, apparently unmoved by the entire

affair, was allowed to give her evidence in writing. Her statement read:
    They had an argument and he was threatening mother. He said he would kill her and hurt daddy, grandma and me. He said he had ways of doing it. My mother was very frightened. I went down to the kitchen and got the knife. I took the knife up to the room in case he hurt mother. I rushed into the room and stuck him with the knife. He screamed.

The jury returned a verdict of justifiable homicide — effectively acquitting Cheryl of blame for the killing.

A friend of Stompanato leaped up in the public gallery and shouted: 'It's lies, all lies. The girl was in love with him, as well. He was killed because of jealousy between mother and daughter.'

The scandal had no ill-effects on Lana's career. *Peyton Place* played to packed houses and she earned an incredible $2 million from her next film, *Imitation Of Life*. But she never got her Oscar. The dramas on the screen never lived up to her most amazing real-life romance and tragedy.

Lana Turner after her daughter's arrest

Sarah Miles

The turbulent, often troubled life of acclaimed film actress Sarah Miles has been remarkable for the controversy her outspoken attitudes have engendered. For she learned at an early age just how to make a name for herself. . . .

Sarah was a pupil at Roedean, the exclusive English school for the well-bred daughters of well-heeled parents. In 1957 the Queen Mother visited the school and, walking down a line of prim young ladies, asked the 14-year-old Sarah: 'And do you like Roedean?' Curtsying, she replied politely but firmly: 'No, ma'am, I hate it!' She was expelled that afternoon.

The incident marked the beginning of Sarah's acting career. She went from Roedean to the Royal Academy of Dramatic Art — and embarked on what appeared to be a shock campaign. By her own admission, she had to wash a lot of men out of her hair after she left home to live with a boyfriend at the age of 17. When they split up, there was a long succession of other loves. But, according to Sarah, 'none of them made any impact'.

She said: 'The trouble was that they all wanted the same thing. They wanted to possess me body and soul — and I couldn't stand that. They all did the wrong things. They spoiled me, did the housework, fawned all over me, demanded to marry me, waited on me hand and foot. And suffocated me. I can't stand that sort of smother love, yet for some reason I seem to attract it.'

Sarah eventually found a stable relationship with playwright Robert Bolt, 18 years her senior. For a while she settled down to the life of an English gentlewoman in their 12-room Georgian mill house. But the appeal of rural life palled — and Sarah found herself straight back on the front pages.

In 1973 the actress was making a film in Arizona with co-stars Burt Reynolds and Lee J. Cobb. Her husband was not involved in the movie, a Western entitled *The Man Who Loved Cat Dancing*, and the actress was accompanied on the US trip by her business manager David Whiting.

On the night of 10 February Sarah went out to dinner with Lee J. Cobb. She returned to the motel in the town of Gila Bend, where most of the cast were staying, and visited Burt Reynolds in his room. When she returned to her own room Whiting was waiting for her.

He demanded to know where Sarah had been and with whom. Unhappy with her explanation, he launched into an enraged torrent of abuse and attacked her, hitting her on the face. She fled back to Burt's room, where she spent the rest of the night.

The following day she returned to her own motel room and found David Whiting lying on the floor — dead from a drugs overdose.

The headlines were sensational. The actress denied that anything but a platonic relationship existed between herself and Reynolds, but the strange circumstances of the suicide were enough to set tongues wagging.

Sarah effectively wrote one of the headlines herself when she revealed to reporters that Whiting had previously threatened to commit suicide and had told her: 'Nobody but me knows how to die of love.'

The publicity did not help her marriage and, when she and Bolt finally separated, Sarah moved from Britain to Los Angeles. Her film career continued, but it was her outspoken views on sex that made the American public sit up and take notice.

She told an American reporter: 'I've never been a prostitute but it's better than working in a factory.' On another occasion she was reported as saying: 'Making love was glorious from the moment I started when young, and I've spent an awful lot of time doing it.'

She was once asked to nominate one man for a night of sex. She replied: 'Hitler.'

Strangely, her own explanation for her desire to shock was that she was intensely shy and nervous of strangers — all of which, she said, 'comes out in aggression and saying outrageous things'.

Her mother, however, had an alternative explanation. Sarah 'does it to make herself more interesting,' she said.

The actress's explicit sex scenes in films such as *Ryan's Daughter* also made her family blush. Her very first nude scene, in *The Servant*, was regarded as something of a milestone in the history of screen nakedness. Her family were dubious — until they read the reviews.

But scenes in a much later film, *The Sailor Who Fell From Grace With The Sea*, went several stages further. That film contained what at the time were said to be some of the most frankly photographed love scenes ever shown in a non-porn movie.

For those who may not have wished to see the entire film, Sarah, then 34, and her co-star Kris Kristofferson re-enacted the most explicit scenes for the camera of *Playboy* magazine. The roles they played were naked, acrobatic and extremely erotic. The pictures caused shock waves around the world and did nothing to cement Kristofferson's marriage to singer Rita Coolidge.

Sarah took it all in her stride. Explaining why she made the film, and why she was happy to re-create the scenes for *Playboy*, she said: 'I am fascinated by erotica, as I am appalled by pornography. Eroticism is rejoicing in love. I believe these love scenes are a rejoicing.

'Eroticism should make you feel warm and good. Bodies intertwined are beautiful. With pornography it's different; it leaves a bad taste in your mouth.'

Koo Stark

When the Queen's second son, handsome, dashing helicopter pilot Prince Andrew, met and fell for a pretty young starlet, the press pursued the couple through every formal function, midnight party and secret assignation of their youthful affair. When 'Randy Andy' and girlfriend Koo Stark went on holiday together the prurient guardians of public morals went berserk. When they stayed together under the same roof, eager newshounds assiduously recorded every minute of the long night watch. It was, after all, the very stuff that makes popular newspapers.

But the greatest scoop of all was when, in 1983, reporters turned up some of the less savoury aspects of Koo's career. For the 25-year-old actress had some embarrassing secrets hidden away in her old film files. Details of her roles in soft-porn movies — illustrated by steamy film stills — were soon spattered across every front page.

Like many actresses before and since, Koo came to regret with bitterness her spicy film past.

At the age of 17, Koo appeared in the sex romp *Emily*, in which she played a virgin staying at an English country house in the twenties. After meeting a young American at dinner, she was shown wriggling about in bed alone as she fantasized about him. Later she enjoyed an explicit lesbian romp, complete with groans of delight, in the shower with a deep-voiced lady artist. Finally there was a no-holds-barred sex scene in the woods with a college student.

Koo went on to make an even hotter film with a then little-known actor, Anthony Andrews, who later became famous for his starring role in the TV series *Brideshead Revisited*. Titled *The Adolescent*, it portrayed Koo as a schoolgirl lured by a porn gang to a bedroom decked out with hidden cameras. In a full-frontal scene, she lost her virginity to Andrews.

The rude wriggling of Koo and Andrews was nothing to their awkward squirming when reminded of such roles. 'I wish I had never done them,' said Koo ruefully — a sentiment echoed by a host of stars who all made films they thought had been forgotten, until they were dug out years later.

Joanna Lumley, who starred in television's *The Avengers* and *Sapphire And Steel*, discovered that the script shown to an inexperienced young actress often bears little resemblance to the final product.

She found that out after making *The Games That Lovers Play* which was reissued years later. Joanna said: 'The film was a comedy and I did take my top off. But the scene was dropped into a later compilation film with bits of soft porn around it. I'm much wiser now.'

Koo Stark, Prince Andrew's former girlfriend

Jackie Bisset, British-born Hollywood star, romped through a torrid love scene in a film called *Secrets* back in 1971. During it she revealed more than she had originally planned. Ten years later Jackie, by now famous, found that the film was being re-released — and protested that her nakedness in it was entirely accidental. She said: 'I was having a simulated love scene with a towel around me. During the shooting I fell out of bed and lost my covering. I showed far more than I meant to and, unknown to me, the cameras kept on rolling.'

Acclaimed actress Diane Keen, who made her name in wholesome British television series like *The Cuckoo Waltz* and *Shillingbury Tales*, made a film in 1974 called *The Sex Thief*, which contained a nude scene which haunted her ever after. She said: 'Times were pretty hard and this was a comedy which I am not ashamed at having made. But it was bought by a company which drafted in other actresses to make it look as if I was doing erotic things from start to finish. It became incredibly filthy.'

Sultry Susan George's fame was enhanced by controversial film love scenes. But she was often very unhappy with the end product. She once said: 'The worst directors are the ones who say "Darling, I don't want you to show a thing." Most of them can't wait for you to get 'em off!'

Well-known comedy star Pamela Stephenson gained a reputation for being outrageous. But even she came to regret the topless scenes in *Stand Up Virgin Soldiers* and the love scenes with Jack Jones in *The Comeback*. She said: 'I'm no prude but I do feel a bit ripped off. I had some good lines in films — but they all ended up on the cutting-room floor.'

Ann Turkel, beautiful ex-wife of actor Richard Harris, claimed that trickery was used to make it appear that she performed in a porno-graphic movie. She said the makers photographed another girl's body for explicit sex scenes.

Joan Crawford, who died in 1977, made a saucy film in which she undressed and indulged in love play with several naked men. She confessed when she signed a contract with MGM, and studio boss Louis B. Mayer bought up all the copies to preserve her image as a family star.

Veteran actress Hedy Lamarr appeared in the cinema's first completely nude scene when she was 16. She played a water nymphette in *Extase 33*, filmed in her native Austria. The shots were innocent by today's standards, but she was so embarrassed by them that she and her husband tried to buy up all prints.

And as a teenage star, Brooke Shields had to battle through the courts to try to prevent nude pictures of herself being published. The shots of her, covered only in oil in a bathtub, were taken when she was just 10.

Marvin Gaye

He was blessed with a smouldering sexuality that women found irresistible and a voice which earned him a place in pop history. Sadly, though, Marvin Gaye was on a self-destruct fuse that no one could make safe. He reached the highest peaks in a glittering musical career, and plumbed the lowest depths of degradation in his obsession with hard drugs. In the end, on the eve of his 45th birthday, he was shot dead by his own father, who later told lawmen of the 'man possessed' his son had become.

Marvin was born in Washington on 2 April 1939 — a date, which he liked to boast to his sexual conquests, was the birthdate two centuries earlier of history's greatest lover, Casanova. The son of a strict Pentecostal preacher, his musical career began when he played his father's organ in church. Then he moved into the choir, where his smooth singing voice needed little professional polishing. He was a natural.

Trouble, however, was not very far away. He had a brief, turbulent spell in the US Army, where he clashed frequently with his superiors. He told them he didn't like the discipline. They responded by slapping charges on him. He was later to say to friends that it was the most miserable time of his life.

After army days it was a succession of small-time groups, dabbling between black soul music, rock 'n' roll and blues. It wasn't until 1963, when he had a hit with *Stubborn Kind of Fellow*, that he found fame — and the trappings of it that were to surround him more in scandal than with glamour.

Closest to him at this time, the start of his heady rise to fame through the celebrated Motown organization, was Tammi Terrell, with whom he formed a deep bond both on and off stage. Together the pair enjoyed ten Top 100 hits, four of them top-ten numbers. He also sang with Diana Ross, Mary Wells and Kim Weston. But his greatest moment of fame came in 1968 with his classic solo version of *I Heard It Through The Grapevine*.

Never one to hide his light under a bushel, Marvin shocked not only his deeply religious parents but America's moral crusaders with his statements at the time about his sexual prowess. 'I am a legitimate sex symbol,' he would say. 'I attract the opposite sex strongly. I always have done. I don't have to work hard to make my records sexy — it just comes naturally.' He flaunted his virile image. Reporters told of interviewing the crooner while he reclined in the afternoon on a bed bigger than his ego, surrounded by gorgeous girls in various states of undress.

Marvin was married to Anna Gordy, the sister of his boss at Motown, Berry Gordy, but fidelity never ranked very high with him. Hollywood buzzed with stories of his sexual prowess; he had moved to Los Angeles . . . and into the drugs scene. He dabbled with cocaine and cannabis, unaware that they were to become major influences on his life, making him unreliable, arrogant and boastful. It was the influence of drugs that led him to make outrageous statements such as: 'The only thing between Beethoven and me is time.'

Then came the greatest tragedy in his life. In 1970 Tammi Terrell collapsed and died in his arms on stage. It shattered him, and for six years after her death he wouldn't play live on stage. His marriage broke up, he slid further into hard-drug abuse, culminating in an attempt to kill himself by taking an overdose of cocaine.

He fought back, remarried, and got back into his music, but then the parting with his second wife Jan — who left him for singer Teddy Prendergrass — plunged him into another fit of depression. He shaved his hair, dabbled in mystic religion, squandered his money at an alarming rate and fled to England in 1980, leaving a £2 million tax bill in America.

Then, in Britain, he committed the ultimate sin: standing up royalty at a special cabaret night. The surly Gaye said he was too exhausted to sing before the audience at a Surrey country club where the special guest was Her Royal Highness Princess Margaret. His boss threatened him on pain of death to make the venue, but by the time he sauntered along, the princess had left — and Gaye was castigated by the newspapers. Where had all the old magic gone? they asked.

Shortly after, he quit Motown, leaped to Number 13 in the British charts in 1982 with *Sexual Healings* — and was on the way to clearing his massive alimony debts.

Then came the night of 1 April 1984 when Marvin Gaye senior, 71, confronted the son he said was 'possessed' . . . and ended his life with two bullets in the chest. His grieving father was to say afterwards: 'He was high on drugs. I shot my son in self-defence.

'Marvin was like a man possessed.'

So ended the black singer's life. He was mourned by a galaxy of Hollywood stars at a funeral the like of which had not been seen since the days of the movie legends.

Almost 30,000 people, some of whom had waited up to 12 hours, flocked to pay tribute at the Los Angeles chapel. One of the cards bore a simple message from megastar Diana Ross — simply saying 'Love.'

For taking his son's life, Marvin Gaye, man of God, was put on probation for five years.

CHAPTER 3

Minding Your Own Business

Prince Bernhard
Bernie Cornfeld
Roberto Calvi
John DeLorean

Judah Binstock
John Stonehouse
Emil Savundra

Prince Bernhard

The people of Holland, thrifty and hard-working, had good reason to be proud of the Dutch royal family, Queen Juliana and her husband, Prince Bernhard.

The queen, one of the richest women in the world, was a benign figurehead in a parliamentary democracy, who often used her own immense wealth to avoid calling on public money to carry out her royal functions.

Her husband, the prince, was a dashing figure who brought more than a touch of glamour to the royal household. During World War II he and his young wife, then a princess, had escaped the German advance into the Netherlands and had led the Dutch Free Forces continuing the fight from British soil. A daring RAF pilot, he returned home as Dutch commander-in-chief to accept the Nazi surrender. In peacetime, he became an energetic businessman, serving as a director of many companies, always striving to promote Dutch commercial interests.

Prince Bernhard never made any secret of the fact that his fees as a business executive were an essential part of his income. The Dutch

Parliament awarded him an annual subsidy of £150,000 to pay for his staff and perform his princely duties, but the Queen herself kept a tight rein on the family finances.

He grumbled in a magazine interview in 1953: 'We princes have financial problems of our own. Like many people these days, we have trouble making ends meet. People think that kings and queens are as rich as the fabled King Midas. It isn't so.' His mild complaints were ignored by loyal Dutch subjects who considered that even royals had to work to earn a living. Senior Dutch politicians greeted his comments with mild amusement, being well aware of the prince's sometimes flamboyant private lifestyle.

But the prince's protestations that he considered himself almost on the breadline were not lost on one group of big spenders who could help solve his financial problems in return for both his support and influence.

In 1959 a glittering prize worth hundreds of millions of pounds was being dangled in front of aircraft manufacturers. That enormous profit depended on their winning the contract to build a new jet fighter for the NATO countries of Europe.

It was a three-horse race, between the British, French and Americans. NATO members such as Germany and Italy, once pioneers in plane-making, had no industry which could deliver the product. 'Junior' members such as Belgium and Holland would also, inevitably, have to choose a foreign-built aircraft.

The Americans were the newcomers to the market, but their brand of high-pressure salesmanship soon left British and French rivals trailing behind. Even inside American industry there was intense competition from different companies, and it was the Lockheed Corporation which made up its mind to win the contract by finding friends in high places.

When the Germans announced they preferred Lockheed's Starfighter jet, it was obvious that a favourable Dutch decision might influence other NATO countries to follow suit.

Prince Bernhard had already been promoting the interests of the American Northrop Tiger fighter, but it had just been ruled out by the Dutch government as too heavy and too expensive.

In 1960, as the crucial decision was about to be taken, the executives of Lockheed in California received a suggestion from their chief European salesman, Dutchman Fred Meuser (a close friend of the royal family), that it would be a public relations triumph to present Prince Bernhard with a new Lockheed Jetstar executive jetliner.

They were still considering the best way of arranging the exorbitant 'gift' when Meuser proposed an alternative. The Prince, he explained, might prefer a payment of the cash value of a Jetstar — about £500,000. The deal was quickly agreed, and the money earmarked for a secret

Prince Bernhard on his 65th birthday

Swiss numbered account. It was the company's biggest single payout of 'commission' in its history.

A few months later, the Dutch government opted to buy the Starfighter and the orders flooded in for Lockheed.

Any strings the prince might have been able to pull had had no influence. The US Department of Defense had tipped the scales in Lockheed's favour by making the Dutch an offer they couldn't refuse — a complete Starfighter squadron thrown in as an 'extra' paid for by the American taxpayers as part of the overseas military aid budget. Regardless of this, Lockheed honoured its offer to the prince with three instalments of money, paid into the Swiss bank.

With his finances brimming from Lockheed's funds, the 'pauper' prince was able to continue his lavish lifestyle in Paris and Rome. But by 1967, as the money was dwindling, Prince Bernhard found himself back in the market for more business 'commissions' — just as Lockheed found themselves once again trying to sell planes to the Dutch government.

The Dutch military officials, seeking a new naval patrol aircraft, had chosen the French Atlantique reconnaissance plane rather than its Lockheed rival, the Orion. However, that decision still had to be ratified by the Dutch parliament. Three Lockheed officials flew to see Prince Bernhard at a friend's apartment in Paris with an offer of £250,000 if he could get the decision reversed in their favour. Bernhard quickly checked with officials in Holland, but had to report with disappointment that there was no way he would bring enough pressure to bear to alter the choice of the French aircraft.

To his delight — and amazement — the Lockheed salesmen promptly insisted on offering a cheque for £50,000 just for trying, and 'to show their appreciation of the prince's honesty'.

In 1973 there seemed to be another opportunity for the prince and Lockheed to do more business. Discussions had begun again in Holland about a further order for naval patrol aircraft, and this time Prince Bernhard wrote to the Lockheed bosses offering his services to help promote the deal. The Lockheed executives studied the prince's letter and concluded that they could end up paying him a commission of around £2 million if they accepted his help. They turned him down.

Angered by the rebuff, Bernhard wrote to Lockheed warning: 'I feel a little bitter and I will do no more for the company.'

Anxious Lockheed officials were sent to soothe the prince's feelings and to offer him another deal — a commission of £500,000 if four Lockheed aircraft were purchased. But the whole arrangement came to nothing. There were unexpected cuts in the Dutch defence budget and no aircraft were bought, American or otherwise.

Prince Bernhard's two letters to Lockheed remained safely hidden in the company confidential files until 1975, when the controllers of

Lockheed had to appear before a Senate committee hearing in Washington to plead their case for a government guaranteed loan to save them from bankruptcy. The senators discovered that the company had spent some £11 million in bribes and kickbacks, and they released details of the payments to Prince Bernhard.

The scandal almost brought down the Dutch monarchy. Within a few days a Dutch judicial commission began their own investigation and Prince Bernhard was forced to resign all his public posts. It was, he told friends later, the worst moment in his life, as bad as an incident during the war when friendly forces had mistakenly opened fire on him as he flew his aircraft in to land at Curaçao Air Base in the Dutch West Indies.

'That burst of fire almost finished me,' he said. 'It was a 21-gun salute with live ammunition.' And the aircraft which survived the salvo of anti-aircraft fire, he recalled fondly, was a twin-engined Lockheed bomber.

Ivar Kreugar

Ivar Kreugar desperately wanted to be known as the world's sharpest businessman. He controlled dozens of international companies and, from his headquarters in Sweden, more than half of the world's match supply.

Kreugar was known as the 'match king', and his empire had been won by ruthless business methods. He bought out or crushed all competitors. A firm that resisted his offer would find its supplies cut off — or its workers beaten up.

By the 1920s Kreugar was living a flamboyant lifestyle, with powerboats, villas, fast cars and mistresses in almost every capital in Europe. His Stockholm headquarters was a massive palace with marble columns and fountains.

Then the Wall Street stock market crash of 1929 dried up the supply of investors' money, and suddenly the bills began to be unpaid. Shares in Kreugar's companies nosedived, despite the millions of pounds of personal cash which he poured in to try to keep prices high.

In a final attempt to raise funds he tried to sell one of his biggest companies to the giant American-owned ITT corporation. They went through the books and announced that £7 million was missing. When the news broke, everyone wanted their money out of Kreugar's companies. Much of it turned up in Swiss bank accounts — under Kreugar's own name.

Hearing that the Swedish Bank was investigating one of his phoney deals involving forged Italian bonds, the 'match king' travelled to his Paris apartments and shot himself through the heart.

Bernie Cornfeld

Who could resist the sales pitch? It took the form of one simple, blunt, direct question. 'Do you sincerely want to be rich?'

The question was posed by a small, tubby American ex-school-teacher, Bernie Cornfeld, one of the smoothest, brightest and most successful salesmen the world of finance has ever seen.

In 95 countries around the world more than 100,000 investors answered Cornfeld with a resounding 'Yes', and they eagerly parted with their savings to put him at the head of IOS: Investors Overseas Services, a mammoth insurance-investment fund which controlled more than £1 billion in stocks and shares.

The IOS sales force, men and women earning colossal fees in commissions for enrolling more subscribers, numbered more than 10,000. And they were all exhorted to outsell each other, to earn the sort of money which would let them live in the same unashamed luxury as their wild-spending boss.

For the top-selling sales representatives there were all-expenses paid trips to sales conferences at the best hotels in Switzerland, the French Riviera and California, where they were showered with large cheques and urged to sign up more investors. Selling shares in IOS and investing in IOS had only one objective — to make you rich, rich, rich.

For a select few who appeared to have the makings of super sales-people, there were visits to Cornfeld's own estates, his palace on Lake Geneva, his French château and his Beverly Hills mansion, where they could witness first-hand all the trappings of fabulous wealth which could be theirs if they tried hard enough.

Cornfeld himself loved nothing more than to show off his 'harem' of 20 beautiful girlfriends who lived in his exotic homes and to display his stables of racehorses and expensive cars. He boasted of his romantic friendships with international glamour girls.

The message to sales staff was clear. If they could sell as well as Bernie, they could live just like him.

In 1965, when he formed IOS in Switzerland, Cornfeld was legally defying American and British financial laws designed to control citizens who wanted to invest in foreign companies. His syndicate guaranteed them the secrecy of the Swiss banking system and very little bureaucratic control over declaring the source of dividends and earnings to their own national tax inspectors.

His first clientele of willing investors came from the hundreds of thousands of US servicemen stationed in Germany who wanted to build up a nest-egg from their pay and overseas allowances. He quickly recruited many of them as part-time sales agents. Within five years the assets of IOS were spread among investments which included oil prospecting, electronics, insurance and goldfields. Some were profitable, some lost money.

Cornfeld's personal stake in IOS made him worth £100 million. But there were two storm clouds on the horizon. IOS had to keep expanding at a near impossible rate to keep paying its sales commissions — and the respectable Swiss authorities were becoming scandalized by Cornfeld's lifestyle.

The bubble burst in 1970 when many of the investors began to share the growing concern of international bankers that IOS was just too good to be true. There were worries that its assets were being mismanaged, and that much of its wealth existed only on paper. At an angry meeting of shareholders Cornfeld was removed from control and the Swiss authorities began fraud investigations into the conduct of IOS. Cornfeld was outraged. As trust in IOS faded rapidly, his own share value dwindled to a mere £4 million.

There was a surge of confidence when another American financial expert took over IOS as president and began a ruthless policy of translating its far-flung assets into hard, tangible cash. Little was known of the new boss: dour, taciturn Robert Vesco, a hard-headed businessman who lived an almost spartan life in complete contrast to Cornfeld's wild existence. By 1973 (when Cornfeld was leading the humble life of an inmate in a Swiss jail, facing fraud charges) Vesco had salvaged some £150 million in IOS cash.

The gratitude of the shareholders was short-lived. Robert Vesco, the poker-faced accountant elected to salvage the savings of IOS investors, vanished. So did most of the money.

He didn't remain hidden for long. Within a few years his own outrageous lifestyle was to eclipse any of Cornfeld's flamboyant fripperies. As Cornfeld was released from jail, without any charges being pressed against him, it became obvious that Vesco's spending spree was unstoppable.

A Senate committee in Washington DC, investigating the scandals of the infamous Watergate affair, heard that Vesco had made an illegal contribution of £100,000 to the campaign funds to re-elect President Richard Nixon, apparently in an attempt to have American government investigators prevented from examining his takeover of IOS.

A warrant was issued for his arrest in 1974, but even the combined resources of the FBI and the CIA were unable to reach him. He fled to Panama, the Bahamas and Costa Rica, among other world-wide sanctuaries from justice.

For many IOS investors there was little they could do but suffer in silence. Thousands of them had broken the laws of their own countries by getting involved in currency dealings to raise the cash to buy IOS shares and they did not dare to admit it.

Others refused to take their losses lying down. They achieved a token success in May 1974 when jet pilot Alwyn Eisenhauer undertook ›a cheeky mission to seize at least some of their money back from Vesco. Dressed in his flying uniform, Eisenhauer appeared at an airport in Panama and angrily ordered the startled ground crew to refuel Vesco's private Boeing 707 airliner to take his 'boss' on a sudden business trip. Surrounded by armed guards at his villa near the airport, Vesco saw his plane roar into the air and vanish northwards. The pilot landed in the United States and calmly claimed his bounty when it was sold for £5 million to help pay the creditors.

Since then the fugitive financier has never appeared in public. And it seems certain that his wealth has grown even greater through business dealings in the Caribbean.

In 1981 Vesco was deported from the Bahamas — and American intelligence officers claimed that he had found a new and bizarre hiding place. They said that the arch-capitalist had moved to a safe haven in Fidel Castro's communist Cuba.

Roberto Calvi

There was an incident during one of the battles of World War II which gave a clue to the hidden personality of banker Roberto Calvi.

As a 22-year-old lieutenant with a cavalry unit of the Italian Army fighting a losing battle alongside their German allies on the Russian Front in 1942, the shy young conscript faced imminent disaster on all sides. His soldiers in full retreat and in danger of dying of starvation, Calvi smooth-talked a suspicious peasant farmer into accepting a promissory note for the value of a stable of horses to replace the steeds his troops had lost in battle.

Out of sight of the gullible farmer, Calvi's men butchered and ate the horses and survived to make their way home safely to Italy. For the ambitious university economics student, it was a perverse lesson in the power of plausible lying. Sometimes bluff brought positive results. As for honouring an IOU, let tomorrow take care of itself.

Forty years later Roberto Calvi was to find out that, sooner or later, a debt has to be settled.

After the war Calvi had resumed his steady rise in the banking establishment, finally becoming chairman of the prestigious Banco Ambrosiano, a Milan finance house which had been founded about

100 years before. It had been nicknamed 'The Priests' Bank' because its founders, devout Catholic merchants, had always refused to compete against profiteering commercial banks. However, behind the respectable façade of the Banco, Calvi was as profit conscious as any of his non-religious rivals.

In the late seventies conditions in Italy were ripe for any money manipulator who had the know-how to cheat the new left-wing government's tight currency restrictions — brought in to halt damaging speculation against the lira, and to prevent money being salted away abroad. Calvi wasted no time setting up his own overseas banking branches in the discreet tax havens of Switzerland, the Bahamas and Panama to spirit money out of the country as secured loans to profitable foreign companies which would repay them later. These companies existed only on paper. They were secretly owned by Calvi, and the loans were used to buy more Ambrosiano shares, giving him more hidden control over the bank.

Three unlikely participants – unwitting and otherwise – were made use of in the Calvi plan.

The first was Michael Sindona, a Sicilian entrepreneur who needed an international network to handle the proceeds of his many shady business deals. Sindona (later to be convicted and jailed in the United States for his own bank swindle) introduced Calvi to two other clients for his overseas banking system.

One of these was 60-year-old Chicago-born Archbishop Paul Marcinkus, a burly cleric who acted as the Pope's bodyguard — and the head of the Vatican Bank. The archbishop, answerable only to the Pope himself, had the job of earning the Church much-needed income on its assets of £1 billion in properties and investments. Marcinkus, who issued temporary 'letters of comfort' guaranteeing the stability of some of Calvi's foreign 'companies', often insisted to sceptical Vatican religious leaders: 'You can't run a Church on Hail Marys alone.'

The most important of Calvi's contacts for clearing his 'hot' money was Licio Gelli, a wealthy Italian businessman with a network of powerful friends around the world. He was grandmaster of Rome's right-wing Freemason's Lodge P.2, with members in almost every level of Italian government. He had enrolled Calvi as a member, guaranteeing him the loyalty and protection of his lodge brothers. In his oath of loyalty, Calvi acknowledged that betrayal of the masonic secrets meant his ritual murder . . . 'having my tongue torn out and being buried in the sand at low water's mark, or a cable length from the shore where the tide ebbs and flows. . . .'

It is unlikely that Calvi and Gelli ever discussed the dark origins of the masons and the likeness of their rituals to those of the black-cloaked London monks who gave their name to Blackfriars Bridge.

It was to Gelli that Calvi turned for help in 1978 when the investigators of the financial controlling body, the Bank of Italy, wanted to look closely at the books of Calvi's bank. Possibly due to Gelli's influence, the investigations soon petered out. Calvi was both impressed and extremely relieved. But that relief was, however, only temporary.

In March 1981 Milan magistrates were interrogating an Italian-American businessman suspected of helping financier Sindona. The suspect revealed that he had visited the home of masonic grandmaster Gelli for his help.

When police raided Gelli's textile factory, the masonic master had already left for South America. However, in his safe they found the membership list of P.2. There were 962 names, including cabinet ministers, heads of the military and secret service, police commissioners and magistrates. And Calvi.

In his prison cell awaiting trial, Calvi blurted out to prosecuting officials many of the secrets of his dealings with the Vatican and the masonic lodge. He was found guilty of currency swindles and sentenced to four years' imprisonment. But he was freed on appeal and, amazingly, was welcomed back at the bank and reinstated.

For the next eleven months Calvi worked furiously to cover up his tracks, and dreamt up wild schemes to try to replace the £800 million in foreign loans he knew would never be repaid. He pleaded with Archbishop Marcinkus at the Vatican to extend the guarantees or to help repay some of the money. He was turned down flat.

At the end of May 1982, using a forged passport, Calvi fled to London and went into hiding in a small rented apartment in Chelsea. He seemed confident that old friends and contacts would help him.

Before he fled he told his own lawyers that he had channelled $50 million to the outlawed Polish trade union movement Solidarity, a cause close to the heart of Pope John Paul. And he claimed he had provided the P.2 lodge with funds to bribe leading political figures throughout Italy and Europe. Calvi warned: 'A lot of people have a lot to answer for. If the whole thing comes out it will be enough to start World War III.'

On 17 June 1982 Calvi vanished from the apartment in Chelsea. The next morning his body was found hanging from scaffolding under Blackfriars Bridge in the heart of London, with the ebb and flow of the tide of the Thames washing round his feet. His body was weighted with stones in his pockets.

An inquest at first decided that Roberto Calvi had committed suicide. At a later hearing this was changed to an 'open' verdict. The jury could not decide with any certainty who had taken Roberto Calvi's life.

The IOU had finally been called in for the man known as 'God's Banker'.

John DeLorean

John Zachary DeLorean was a daring and imaginative businessman who promised to help end some of the misery of unemployment in Northern Ireland by bringing in the British taxpayer as a partner in a dynamic new project building a revolutionary advanced sports car which would set the pioneering pace for the personal road transport of the future.

But then John DeLorean was always full of promises — and very little else.

He was the Hollywood image of a successful tycoon, 1.93 metres (6ft 4ins) tall, with a handsomely mature head of elegant silver hair and a tough manly jaw. There was never any doubt that he believed in himself, and his greatest asset was his ability to persuade others to share that belief.

His career background was, at first glance impressive. The son of an immigrant couple, DeLorean had been born and brought up in Detroit. He had graduated from a music scholarship before being lured into a job with General Motors, the ailing car giant which was looking for fresh talent.

By the mid 1960s, through a mixture of teamwork and inspiration, the Pontiac division of General Motors, where DeLorean worked, had broken away from producing sedate saloon cars and instead turned out the sleek, high-powered Pontiac GTO, a speedy grand-touring Ferrari lookalike which captured the imagination of the American car-buying public on a gigantic scale and made Pontiac the most profitable division in the General Motors empire.

John DeLorean, who took credit for the entire concept, looked as if he couldn't put a foot wrong. However, promoted to run General Motors biggest division, Chevrolet, the enterprising DeLorean was cut off from the unsung heroes of the team of engineers who had devised the successful GTO. His flood of creative ideas was reduced to a trickle.

If John DeLorean ever sensed the growing disappointment of his employers, he never let it show. He simply set about changing his own image to resemble that of the sporty GTO which had brought him such prestige. He went on a crash diet to achieve a slim, athletic look, and invested in a major facelift, including a plastic insert in his cheeks to give him that forceful jutting jawline.

By the end of the sixties DeLorean was running out of excuses to General Motors for his lack of inventiveness. He blamed a new American consumer concern about safety and fuel efficiency for the slump in car sales but he couldn't come up with any fresh designs for a car to satisfy those new customer demands. There was also growing criticism that he was using company expense accounts to support his increasingly expensive private life and his lavish courtship of beautiful model Christine Ferrare, 30 years his junior and shortly to become his third wife.

In 1973 the executives of General Motors hired a team of private detectives to examine DeLorean's flamboyant lifestyle, with particular emphasis on sensitive commercial secrets which were being leaked. Soon afterwards the president of the company summoned DeLorean and asked him to resign.

With wounded pride, he promised he would build his own car empire, big enough to rival even General Motors itself. Almost overnight he announced that he had designs for a new car which would be safe, fuel-efficient, and last a lifetime. It was, he said, the car which Detroit would not build because it didn't fit into their market strategy of cars which fell apart every few years and had to be replaced with new models.

After five years living off his dwindling savings, DeLorean could still find no one in the United States to put money behind his faded reputation. So he turned further afield. He received responses of mild interest from the Irish Republic and from Puerto Rico, who both offered him free factory sites and tax concessions but no hard cash. Much more receptive was the British government, anxious to inject some prosperity into Northern Ireland, which had the highest unemployment rate in Western Europe.

A preliminary check on DeLorean's reputation in the United States seemed to back up his claims. It was true he had produced massive profits for General Motors with the Pontiac GTO, and that he had quarrelled with them about producing a new economical, safe car for the 1980s. Deeper questioning, however, would have shown that DeLorean never had the answer then — and still did not.

DeLorean pressed London for a quick decision, and in August 1978 the British government announced that they were giving him £54 million to build a factory just outside Belfast.

DeLorean claimed he had already hundreds of would-be dealers in the United States clamouring to pay to secure the exclusive rights to sell the new cars in the American markets. When the foundations were being laid for the factory, he proudly announced: 'As of now we have advance orders for 30,000 cars.' Those advance orders — which would have guaranteed years of profitability as soon as the factory opened — were just a figment of DeLorean's imagination.

By February 1981 the factory complex was complete, and in the next ten months more than 8,300 of the sports cars, with their glistening stainless-steel bodies and gull-wing doors, roared off the production lines.

John DeLorean at the Earl's Court Motorfair, 1981

John DeLorean breathed a sigh of relief. He needed some income passing through the company bank accounts to disguise the fact that millions of pounds of British taxpayers' money had already seemingly evaporated.

DeLorean had gambled on the fact that you can fool some of the people all of the time — civil servants, book-keepers and long-suffering taxpayers being amongst the most gullible. But you can't fool the car-buying public, who want to kick the tyres and rattle the wheels before they part with their hard-earned cash. Lured by a massive advertising campaign, they flocked to see the new car. They took it for a test drive and then brought it back to the dealers without buying it.

Engineered and designed in an impossibly short space of time to match the impatient ambitions of John DeLorean, the car was uneconomical, underpowered, unreliable and unwanted.

Thousands of the cars were stockpiled in the showrooms and at Belfast docks because no American customers could be found for them. By summer of 1982 Renault, who supplied the engines, were threatening to put the company into liquidation unless they were paid their outstanding bills.

John DeLorean had promised 30,000 firm orders for the cars. Only 3,347 of them had been sold. Finally, with £30 million more invested, an embarrassed British government appointed receivers to take control of the company and began to organize an investigation by fraud squad detectives.

DeLorean's only hope was to raise some fast money to pay off the creditors and get himself back in the driving seat. That was when he found himself involved in a market much more profitable than building and selling cars.

In June 1982 he had received a sympathetic phone call from James Hoffman, a former neighbour in California, and the two old friends began discussing how £25 million could be raised to prevent the complete collapse of DeLorean's enterprise. Little did the slick-talking car salesman realize he was dealing with a drug smuggling informer for the FBI.

He found out the truth four months later when he met Hoffman in room 501 of the Sheraton Plaza hotel in downtown Los Angeles. Unaware that the room was bugged with microphones and hidden cameras, the man the British government had trusted with £84 million of public money sat beside a suitcase full of cocaine.

While Hoffman promised him that a small investment in the deadly drug would reap him millions in profits, John DeLorean, the tycoon who would never admit failure, handled a plastic package of cocaine and laughed: 'It's better than gold. Gold weighs more than that, for God's sake.'

His smile faltered uncertainly a few moments later when a tall stranger entered the room and greeted him: 'I'm Jerry West, I'm with the FBI. You are under arrest for narcotics law violation.'

The FBI handcuffs, the same glittering stainless steel as the bodywork of his ill-fated sports car, were snapped firmly round DeLorean's well-manicured hands.

He was charged with conspiracy to distribute £15 million worth of cocaine. The jury who heard his case in Los Angeles almost two years later were faced with a John DeLorean who looked gaunt and haggard. They decided after a 62-day trial that DeLorean, a desperate man, had been trapped into a crime he never meant to commit by FBI agents and informers who deliberately set out to create that crime. He was acquitted.

Only as he stepped out of the courtroom did he finally face reality. He admitted: 'My career is ruined. Let's face it, would you buy a used car from me?'

Judah Binstock

Judah Binstock's life revolved around three obsessive passions — money, power and sex. And according to business associates and girl-friends, he was never short of any of those commodities.

Elegant, sophisticated women melted in the arms of the overweight London solicitor. Top politicians and senior policemen in London, Lisbon and Los Angeles became restless and uneasy in his presence. Hard-headed businessmen were persuaded to part with millions of pounds, dollars and francs under the spell of his forceful and dynamic personality. When they were left to face the music for a string of deals which brought Binstock a fabulous fortune, they could only plead that he seemed to have the power to 'hypnotize' them.

When the international wheeler-dealer retired to a life of luxury on the Mediterranean, London magistrates issued a fruitless warrant for his arrest in the case of one lucrative crooked deal and concluded: 'The fraud was devised and orchestrated by Judah Binstock. He was the puppet-owner pulling the strings.'

Even ten years after Binstock left British shores to self-imposed exile in Spain, fraud squad detectives at Scotland Yard were still unsure how much money he had made from reputable international companies and the British Treasury.

From his home in Marbella, on the Costa Del Sol, the fugitive businessman threatened: 'If I ever returned to Britain to answer the accusations against me, it will cost them £200 million for a start and uncover a scandal that will tear the City and the Treasury apart. I'll show them.'

He has never made good that threat, to the apparent relief of many influential figures in British politics and banking.

Born to struggling Russian-Jewish refugee parents in the mean surroundings of the East End of London in 1935, Judah Eleazer Binstock made no secret of his ambition to strive for the relative affluence and security of a middle-class lifestyle. He had achieved that comfortably by his late twenties, when he had become a hard-working, modestly successful solicitor. But as his business prospered, so did his appetite for sex and real wealth and the power which went with it.

Binstock's Hungarian first wife, Imata Polyak, was introduced to him by a businesss colleague on the understanding that a £10 debt would be cancelled. Soon after their marriage, she complained that her husband began to demand that she should invite other women to join in their love-making sessions.

Putting pleasure before business, he even insisted on having sex in his office, while important clients were kept waiting in his reception room. But even if the clients were busy men to whom time was money, they were still prepared to wait patiently for an appointment with the solicitor who seemed to have the Midas touch when it came to putting together increasingly profitable property and share deals.

By the mid-sixties he had forsaken his law practice and had become a property tycoon and the principal shareholder in a casino in London. Through his shrewd vetting of membership of the casino, he was able to set up an elaborate network of contacts among leading politicians, businessmen, showbusiness celebrities, prominent police officers and visiting 'financiers' from the United States, who were valuable allies in a series of deals which netted him millions of pounds. In one transaction alone he cleared a profit of £2 million by cornering the market for rice in Italy.

'It's all a question of knowing the right people in the right places,' he boasted. The 'right' people among Binstock's friends were rewarded with lavish gifts and all-expenses-paid invitations to the new £1 million villa which was being built for him in the exclusive Spanish resort of Marbella. Five hundred of them were flown to his new home on chartered jets for a party, with Binstock picking up the bill for their accommodation at nearby luxury hotels. Highly paid courtesans from Paris were flown in for the occasion in an extravagant display of sexual bribes which became a hallmark of Binstock's business techniques.

At one tough negotiating session Binstock had been trying to cajole a German banker into financing a property deal. The German, who had been admiring Binstock's beautiful girl escort, had teased him: 'I will agree to the contract but only if you throw in the girl.' With one nod from Binstock, the girl left his side and immediately joined the new German partner in a sensual embrace. The deal was signed.

By 1969 he was so anxious to expand his business on an international scale, and to avoid potential tax liabilities and scrutiny by British government agencies, that he left England and set up home in Paris with his second wife Patrina.

From then on he commuted regularly to London, being warmly greeted by his inner circle of close associates on his extended business trips, but always returning swiftly home to Paris when warned of fresh investigations into his murky business affairs. He sold off his interest in the London casino after four of his employees were convicted of offences connected with 'profit skimming', and he skilfully avoided inquiries into dubious insurance claims where he had pocketed handsome compensation when the offices of one of his property companies mysteriously caught fire and its records were destroyed.

Operating freely outside Britain, with easy access to his newly established Swiss banking accounts, Binstock sought to entice British investors into financing more property and currency speculation projects in Europe and the United States.

Among those enterprising, respected businessmen who were under Binstock's hypnotic spell was Sir Eric Miller, chairman of the £40 million Peachey Property Corporation, who was later the centre of a suicide scandal because of his involvement with Judah Binstock. Miller and others were only too eager to entrust huge funds to Binstock. But there was one obstacle in their way — the Bank of England.

In order to try to encourage British financiers to invest their wealth in shares in British industry at home, the government had introduced regulations which imposed a hefty burden on those who wanted to convert their pounds into dollars for overseas investments. The 'dollar premium' forced them to pay an additional fee for foreign investment funds. For those who still wanted to struggle under that penalty, 75 per cent of the fee was refundable by the Treasury when the overseas investments were eventually sold off and the money brought back to Britain.

For anyone but Judah Binstock, that would have been a daunting handicap to overcome in luring money out of Britain. But to Binstock it was a challenge. If trusting British businessmen couldn't funnel their money to him, he would make the British government itself pay for putting obstacles in his path.

Under an elaborate smokescreen of bogus paperwork, he began to bring millions of pounds back into Britain. The paperwork seemed to show that the money was overseas investment being 'repatriated', and Binstock brazenly applied for the refund of 'dollar premium' penalties — which had never been paid in the first place.

Horatio Bottomley

Horatio Bottomley went from rags to riches and back to rags again. At one stage of his life he was one of the most respected men in Britain; at another time he was the most despised.

Born in London's East End in 1860, and raised in an orphanage, Bottomley at first worked as a solicitor's clerk and then as a shorthand writer at the Law Courts. He soon switched to the wrong side of the law, however, by setting up companies and selling them at inflated prices to other companies under his control, which then went bankrupt.

Despite his amazingly blatant fiddles, Bottomley found no shortage of investors. He lived the life of a lord at his Sussex home, where his wife was apparently unaware of his string of mistresses up and down the country. He was elected to Parliament to represent the London constituency of Hackney South, and he founded his own fiercely patriotic newspaper, *John Bull.*

In 1912 he suffered a setback when he was forced to resign from Parliament after a particularly scandalous bankruptcy. There was also the suspicion that some of the amazingly generous prizes he was offering in the pages of his newspaper were going straight into his own pocket.

At the outbreak of World War I Bottomley's jingoism suited the mood of the nation. *John Bull* flourished and its publisher threw himself into the war effort, making stirring recruiting speeches around the country for which he charged a not-ungenerous fee.

The voters rewarded his patriotism by re-electing him to his old constituency as soon as the war was over. But a year later his frauds caught up with him.

During the war Bottomley had launched a Victory Bonds Club to help small investors buy a share in the £5 bonds that the government had issued. Half a million pounds flowed in — and Bottomley siphoned off about £150,000 of it. One of his former partners alerted the police, and the flamboyant crook was brought to trial at the Old Bailey. He was jailed for seven years.

Released on licence in 1926, Bottomley started a new newspaper along the lines of *John Bull.* It was titled *John Blunt,* and was as hypocritically tub-thumping as its predecessor. This time the public saw through the publisher's cant, and the journal folded.

In 1933 he started a new career as a concert-hall comedian, but after only a few nights he collapsed from a heart attack. Extraordinarily, the former partner whose evidence had landed him in jail took pity on Bottomley and offered him a home for the rest of his life. Before he could take up the offer, however, he died, a broke and broken man.

He had netted at least £2 million undetected by Treasury experts when his scheme was uncovered by two vigilant Customs officials who stopped him during a routine search at Heathrow Airport in September 1976. As they made a quick examination of his luggage, they noticed him casually toss the torn remains of two sheets of notepaper into a waste bin. They carefully retrieved the scraps and pieced them together.

At first they could make no sense of the crumpled notes, but financial experts who later 'decoded' them found them to be part of the complex jigsaw of fraud, preparations for more paperwork claiming false premium repayments.

Another set of notes were more sinister. They were the draft of a blackmail letter, obviously from a man who feared for his life. Binstock simply claimed he was carrying the letter for an associate who was 'under pressure'.

The letter warned:

I consider I owe nothing to you or your associates (Greek or Floridian). I am not prepared to pay any more and I have taken steps to protect myself if anything untoward happens. A dossier has been prepared which sets out in detail bank statements, cashiers' cheques and evidence of a large transfer of dollars. A number of copies of these have been lodged with certain institutions who have instructions to send them to the US authorities and the Swiss authorities. These files will be sent upon my death or disappearance after a limited time triggered by no communication from me, or any other hostile movement or action.

Judah Binstock has not reappeared in Britain since those letters were discovered. Eighteen months later two officials of a London accountancy firm were fined £200,000 for their part in providing the paperwork for Binstock's fraud, yet the financier himself has remained successfully out of reach of any extradition orders, usually protected by the armed guards of a private security service.

However, the mystery remains of the authorship of the defiant blackmail letter, apparently addressed to one of Binstock's American partners.

Was the writer a harassed and frightened businessman who feared a 'contract' murder because he had refused to keep up payments on some crooked deal? Was the letter connected with the £200 million scandal which Judah Binstock threatened to reveal and 'tear the City and the Treasury apart'? Are there copies of damning dossiers still ready to be sent to American and Swiss treasuries if and when the author dies?

If so, there will be many worried millionaires in London and Miami and Marbella who hope the mystery writer takes care in crossing the road, and lives a long and healthy life.

John Stonehouse

Few politicians make bigger headlines with their death announcement than they manage in their lifetime. But one of Britain's brightest, most dynamic, handsome and promising politicians achieved just that in 1974. The reason for the special interest taken by colleagues, political foes and the press were twofold: firstly, because of the mysterious circumstances surrounding his demise and, secondly, because of the rumours of financial and romantic misbehaviour that preceded it.

The speculation proved to be justified. For the 48-year-old member of parliament whose death was announced in banner headlines in all British newspapers was in fact alive, well and lounging in the sunshine 13,000 miles away.

His name was John Stonehouse, and he almost pulled off the perfect vanishing trick — apparently disappearing from the face of the earth and leaving behind him his constituents, several ailing companies, debts of about £800,000, two children, a wife and a mistress.

John Stonehouse was ambitious for power and greedy for riches. He entered the House of Commons as a Labour MP in 1957, and became a privy councillor, aviation minister, technology minister and eventually postmaster-general. But when Labour lost power in 1970 he turned his hand to more lucrative endeavours to supplement his MP's salary.

In just five years he formed 20 companies, including a merchant bank. None was successful, but trading figures were given a facelift for the benefit of accountants and investors by manipulating funds between one company and another. It was a survival technique that could not last, and in 1974 the Department of Trade began to investigate. All Stonehouse's influence as a former Cabinet minister could not save him. He knew he faced being branded a liar and a cheat, would be ruined and disgraced and might even be prosecuted for fraud.

John Stonehouse decided that he would have to 'die'. Not the sort of man to commit suicide, he would simply run away from his troubles, taking with him as much of his money as he could.

But it was not only money he hoped to take. Stonehouse also planned to take abroad the one ally he felt he could trust implicitly — his secretary, Sheila Buckley.

Mrs Buckley, then 28, had recently divorced her husband, an accountant, after an unhappy three-year marriage. But long before the divorce she had fallen deeply in love with her boss. They had become regular lovers, meeting after the day's Commons business at a bachelor flat Stonehouse kept nearby.

The MP planned a new life for them in New Zealand. It was agreed that he should flee first while his mistress remained in Britain until it was safe to join him. But first of all the most detailed, cunning and sometimes cynical arrangements had to be made to ensure their freedom from discovery.

As MP for Walsall, Staffordshire, Stonehouse tricked a local hospital into giving him details of men of his age who had recently died. With two suitable names, Donald Mildoon and Joseph Markham, he called on the widows and, under the guise of a concerned and caring MP, extracted from them all the information he needed to steal either or both of the dead men's identities.

Using a ruse described by author Frederick Forsyth in his book *Day Of The Jackal,* Stonehouse obtained copies of the dead men's birth certificates. Then, deciding that Markham's was the identity he preferred, he applied for a passport in the deceased's name. He had himself photographed with glasses and a wide grin and countersigned the snapshot on the back in the name of a fellow MP, Neil McBride, whom he knew was dying of cancer. No one at the Passport Office queried the application or the phoney photograph and on 2 August 1974 the cunning MP picked up his brand-new passport.

John Stonehouse and Joseph Arthur Markham were now one and the same person. He could change his identity at will.

In the next three months Stonehouse opened no fewer than 27 bank accounts in his own name in 17 banks, as well as nine accounts in the names of Markham or Mildoon. He flew to Switzerland and deposited large sums in Markham's name. He put further illicit amounts in a London account, then transferred them to the Bank Of New South Wales. He took out several credit cards in Markham's name, provided him with an address at a cheap London hotel and set up a company 'J. A. Markham, export-import consultant' using a business accommodation address.

On 6 November Stonehouse made a dummy run along the first stage of his escape route. He flew to Miami, Florida, posing as Markham, ordering the tickets in his name and paying for them with Markham's American Express credit card. He returned to London a few days later to report to Sheila Buckley that their plan was foolproof. . . .

On 19 November Stonehouse again flew to Miami, this time for a business meeting. He was accompanied by James Charlton, deputy chairman of one of his companies. The following day Stonehouse announced that he was going for a swim and wandered along Miami Beach. He stopped for a long chat with 65-year-old Mrs Helen Fleming, who ran the beach office of the giant Fontainbleau Hotel, gave her his name and wished her well. Having thus established his identity, he strolled down towards the surf — and vanished.

Some hours later his partner reported him missing. His clothes were found on the sand. Miami Beach Police Department sent a message to Scotland Yard: 'John Stonehouse presumed dead.'

By that time the cool conman was safely away. Instead of going for a swim, he had scurried along the beach to a disused building where he retrieved a hidden suitcase containing clothes, money, traveller's cheques and the phoney passport. He took a cab to the airport, flew to San Francisco under Markham's name and transferred to a Hawaii flight. In Honolulu he called his mistress at a quiet London hotel and boasted that the plan had worked.

Stonehouse's assurance was premature, for when on 27 November he arrived in Melbourne, Australia, and began almost immediately to transfer money from an Australian bank account in the name of Mildoon to a New Zealand bank account in the name of Markham, suspicions were aroused.

The banks called the police, and Stonehouse was put under surveillance. The following day suspicions were heightened when the mysterious newcomer flew back to Europe — for a secret meeting in Copenhagen with Sheila Buckley. On 10 December he was back in Melbourne, visiting banks almost daily and transferring funds from one account to another.

Even at that stage Stonehouse might have escaped. But police throughout Australia had been put on the alert for another Englishman on the run: Lord Lucan, who had disappeared after murdering his family's nanny. When Victoria State Police wired Scotland Yard requesting further pictures of the peer, photographs of a second missing Briton were sent along too. The photographs were of John Stonehouse.

On Christmas Eve 1974 'Joseph Markham' was arrested. At first he denied his real identity, but in his pocket was a letter from Sheila Buckley. It said: 'Dear Dums [her pet name for him]. Do miss you. So lonely. Shall wait forever for you.'

Extraordinarily, Stonehouse's first request after admitting his identity was to be allowed to telephone his 45-year-old wife Barbara. Even more extraordinary was what detectives listening on another line heard him say to her . . . 'Come out here as soon as possible — and bring Sheila with you. The poor girl's been going through hell.'

Barbara Stonehouse did fly to her husband's side. So, separately, did Sheila Buckley. The deceived wife soon returned home to institute divorce proceedings but the mistress stayed on in Australia with her lover until in July 1975 Stonehouse was extradited to stand trial in Britain.

The case took months to prepare, at an estimated cost to the taxpayer of £750,000. At the end of a 68-day trial Stonehouse was found guilty of 14 charges involving theft, forgery and fraud. He was jailed for seven years. Sheila Buckley was given a two-year suspended sentence for helping him.

Despite the harm Stonehouse had done her, despite the judge's description of him as an 'extremely persuasive, deceitful and ambitious man', Sheila Buckley stood by him.

He suffered two heart attacks and left jail after serving three years of his sentence, a sick, bankrupt and broken man. He and Sheila moved into a modest flat, and in 1981 they married in a secret country ceremony.

John Stonehouse

Emil Savundra

Emil Savundra never made any secret of the lifestyle he wanted for himself. He enjoyed wallowing in luxury, gorging himself on the richest food and drink, living in an elegant mansion in London's Mayfair, driving his Rolls-Royce to glittering social occasions, escorting beautiful women, thundering through the waves at the helm of his expensive, over-powered ocean speedboat.

'I am God's own lounge lizard,' he admitted, without the slightest trace of guilt. 'I don't like work.'

In the swinging sixties in Britain, he was able to indulge his extravagant tastes to the full and bask in the open admiration of fellow businessmen and grateful customers.

If Emil Savundra had a distaste for physical labour, his agile mind never failed to work overtime to keep cash rolling in to support his lavish spending. His timing was just right. Britain was booming, and everyone seemed to have money in their pockets. Prime Minister Harold Macmillan went on record as saying 'You've never had it so good.'

One sign of the prosperous economy was the growing number of cars rolling off the production lines and on to the roads. Since every driver of those cars needed to be insured, Savundra decided to cash in on an expanding market just ripe for his own personal brand of slick financial salesmanship.

Born in Ceylon in 1923, he had arrived in Britain just in time for the economic boom, leaving behind him a string of disastrous business deals in China, Ghana and Belgium. But Savundra, whose wife was a member of a wealthy, land-owning Sinhalese family, still had just enough cash reserves to set up his own insurance business — Fire, Auto and Marine — in 1963.

His company offered insurance coverage for car drivers at half the premiums they could expect to pay elsewhere. Business took off overnight; as the money poured in Savundra looked set to become an instant success story.

The podgy insurance chief, with his sleek head of silver hair, exuded the charm and assurance of an experienced international businessman. While other ambitious insurance agents tried in vain to match his cut-price rates, Savundra revealed casually: 'My methods are the most modern and cost-effective. Traditional insurance companies need to charge exorbitant fees because their out-of-date system loads them with big overheads and costs. The public is forced by law to have car insurance, and for too long they have been paying inflated premiums to support inefficient businesses.'

Maundy Gregory

A sharp entrepreneur named Maundy Gregory took a leaf out of the book of a prime minister — and ended up in jail for his misdeeds.

Shortly after the end of World War I the Liberal premier, Lloyd George, was openly selling off peerages, knighthoods and other honours in an attempt to bolster his political funds and to ensure a healthy majority of supporters in the House of Lords. Maundy Gregory decided to follow suit.

He first built up his image as a man of influence by launching a patriotic newspaper and by starting his own club for gentlemen and the nobility. Then he set up palatial offices in a building not far from the prime minister's residence in Downing Street, and placed at the door a commissionaire in the uniform of a government messenger.

Through bribery, flattery and lavish gifts, Gregory would discover who among the political and social hierarchy was in line for an honour. Likely candidates would be sent letters suggesting a meeting to discuss 'a matter of great confidence'. Gregory would wine and dine them one by one — and end up by offering to 'ensure' that a particular honour be obtained. He charged up to £50,000 for a peerage, £35,000 for a baronetcy and £10,000 for a knighthood. Many paid his price, unaware that they would have received their honours anyway.

Gregory's reputation spread and in some cases rich businessmen anxious for honours approached him direct. The conman would then have to employ all his charm and influence to have extra names added to the honours list.

When Lloyd George's government fell to the Conservatives, under Stanley Baldwin, Gregory's days of easy money were numbered. An Act of Parliament in 1925 made the trading of honours illegal. A Conservative Party official was infiltrated into Gregory's organization to find out the names of those to whom Gregory had promised titles.

Still the conman continued until, in 1933, he made his first big mistake. He had a letter sent to Commander Edward Leake suggesting a lunch, over which the intrigued military man was offered a knighthood for £10,000. The commander went to Scotland Yard.

Gregory was brought to court, where he at first denied all charges before being prevailed upon to change his plea to guilty. This did away with the need for further evidence — and many people in high places breathed sighs of relief. A long-drawn-out trial could have exposed many people who had bought their titles from Gregory.

The artful fixer was jailed for two months. After his release Gregory survived one more scandal, over the mysterious death of Edith Rosse, the woman he had been living with for some years, before he left the country to live in Paris.

Dr Emil Savundra and his wife Pushpam

It was just the message car drivers wanted to hear. However, Emil Savundra's business methods were far from innovative. They were as old as the history of swindling itself. He was simply robbing Peter to pay Paul. As long as the cash was flowing in, he could use the new income to settle outstanding and overdue debts.

Board of Trade regulations insisted that insurance companies had to build up cash reserves, always ensuring they had money to meet claims by their customers. But as with all insurance business, there was an initial, bountiful period of grace when the premiums were being paid and the claims for losses and damages were not yet being made. It was the time when the cash reserves should have been built up to meet the drain of compensation when it did arise — as it was bound to do sooner or later.

Savundra gave no thought for the days of reckoning which lay ahead. Payments to his company were being made at the rate of £40,000 a week and he used much of that money as his private bank balance, to spend as he wished.

The flamboyant businessman hit the headlines when he entered his powerboat *Jackie S.* (named after his daughter) in an international race in the English Channel. The boat, propelled by four massive Jaguar engines, was a mirror of Savundra's own personality — its runaway power was greater than anyone's ability to control it.

It shot away from the starting line and immediately collided with a rival boat. The crews of both vessels only escaped serious injury by sheer good luck. Trying to catch up with the other competitors, Savundra opened the throttles to full power and *Jackie S.* veered wildly on to the Needles rocks. With the hull still intact, he reversed off the rocks and set off again in hot pursuit, straight into the hull of a 30-foot pleasure boat which split up and sank. Fortunately, the crew had dived overboard to safety seconds before their craft was rammed.

Experienced, more traditional skippers noted with some satisfaction that the brash newcomer had to retire from the race.

It should have been an omen for the businessman whose employees called him 'Caesar'. But Savundra was undaunted. 'Bloody good sport,' was his verdict.

It took only two years for cash claims against Fire, Auto and Marine to begin to outstrip its income. By that time more than £3 million had passed through the books.

At first Savundra tried to stave off the inevitable by ordering his staff to restrict payouts for claims to £10,000 a week. Unpaid claims began to mount into a backlog, ticking away like a time bomb.

When Board of Trade examiners demanded to inspect his accounts to see if his company had sufficient cash reserves to meet its debts, he fooled them and his fellow directors by producing a statement from a Liechtenstein company reassuring the auditors that it held more than half a million pounds worth of British government bonds in the account of Fire, Auto and Marine.

The Liechtenstein 'bankers' were a fake company set up by Savundra to skim money out of the insurance company for his own pocket. Inevitably, by 1966 Fire, Auto and Marine didn't have the money to meet the claims of 400,000 trusting motorists who had paid to be safely insured against damage, death and injury.

As the company collapsed, so did Savundra. He was taken to a London hospital with a heart attack, and later fled to Switzerland and Ceylon for a convalescence which kept him out of reach of Board of Trade investigators.

But Savundra, the optimist, gambled on his belief that he risked only a civil bankruptcy case, not criminal charges, and he returned to London a year later. He drew unemployment benefit and dreamed of other money-making schemes while his company affairs were investigated.

He brazenly accepted the invitation to appear on television to be questioned by interviewer David Frost about the unpaid claims against Fire, Auto and Marine. In the full glare of studio lights he was unmasked as a heartless swindler who spent other people's money without a care for the misery he caused them. Challenged by two women widowed by road accidents caused by drivers insured by Fire, Auto and Marine — compensated with worthless cheques which had bounced — he screamed at them: 'I have no legal or moral responsibility.'

When the studio audience protested, he shouted: 'I do not want to cross swords with peasants.'

The police had to escort him from the studios for his own safety — and the police were never far away for the next year, until Emil Savundra was tried and sentenced to eight years in jail for fraud.

Because of his heart ailment he served only six years.

On his release in 1974 he proposed his most ambitious scheme. In return for 200 million dollars he would let the United States establish a strategic nuclear base on an estate owned by his wife's family. He insisted his wife should be declared queen of North Ceylon. Emil Savundra would become king.

The Americans were soft-hearted enough not to shatter the dreams of a dying man. He never knew his offer had been consigned to the wastebin of crank ideas. Savundra died in 1976 broke, an uncrowned king mourned only by his family.

CHAPTER 4

Embarrassing Revelations

Billie Jean King

To brave scandal for the love of a beautiful woman is one thing: there will always be a certain sympathy for the husband with the roving eye, the wife wooed by a seducer. But world tennis star Billie Jean King endured a scandal which cost her dear in terms of torment from the fickle public. For her love affair was conducted with another woman. Not only was her privacy savaged in the newspapers, but she learned the hard way that even in this so-called age of enlightenment the practice of lesbianism can still evoke bitter passions.

Billie Jean King was a woman on top of the world when the storm broke unexpectedly in 1981. She had won an unequalled 20 titles at Wimbledon in a glittering career as a professional tennis player. Her skill was unrivalled on the famous centre court, where she notched up six singles victory titles and earned the admiration of sportsmen and women everywhere. Her private life too, it was assumed, was as settled and as happy as her tennis career. There had never been any whiff of scandal to dent the 16-year marriage that Billie Jean had enjoyed with husband Larry. In short, life was rosy.

Then, as suddenly as one of her famous serves coming off her racket at phenomenal speed, she was plunged into a terrible crisis. Out of her past came a lesbian lover, claiming money for the soured affair which ended in suicide attempts and two court cases.

Billie Jean was to be spared nothing by the woman scorned.

The woman was Marilyn Barnett, aged 33 in April 1981 when she lodged a lawsuit alleging that she had had a long lesbian affair with Mrs King, 37, while working for her as a secretary and personal assistant. She claimed the rights to a house on beautiful Malibu Beach — which she alleged Mrs King promised her during the affair — and the right to lifetime financial support, which again she said had been promised to her.

In the lawsuit she said she had been a hairdresser when she met Mrs King in 1972 — a job she gave up to become the personal aide and friend of the star. 'I became a secretary, confidante, companion, cook, cleaning person — all the things necessary to allow Mrs King to concentrate on her game.'

The suit claimed that Billie Jean had given her a verbal contract by pledging to meet every monetary need she would encounter for the rest of her life.

Understandably, perhaps, Mrs King rushed to deny the allegations. While pressmen were despatched to track down the wheelchair-bound Miss Barnett — she had broken her back in failed suicide attempts over her lost love — Billie Jean said: 'The allegations are untrue and completely unfounded. I am completely shocked and disappointed.'

Two days later she called a press conference and admitted that she had indeed had a lesbian affair with Miss Barnett. She told reporters 'It's been over for some time. I've always been honest and I have decided to talk to you as I have always talked to you — from the heart.

'I'm very disappointed and shocked that Marilyn has done this not only to herself — a very self-destructive thing — but also to other people who care for her. I now know who my friends are.'

It transpired that the pair had drifted into the liaison when Miss Barnett was indeed hired as secretary. Mrs King was later to admit that she had never thought of herself before as homosexual, but she did not deny that she enjoyed sleeping with Marilyn. She knew, however, that in the fuddy-duddy tennis world — where morals are counted by some to be as important as correct dress and manners on the court — she would be in for a rough ride. That was why, just days after the press conference, she offered to resign her post as president of the Women's Tennis Association — because she didn't want the game that she loved to be harmed.

Marilyn Barnett, meanwhile, through her lawyer, was telling her side of the sorry tale: that she had loved Mrs King, that she 'gave her life' to her, that she envisaged from 1972 onwards always being her lover. 'I gave up my career, my identity, my pride and my home,' she said. 'In return, Billie Jean had always promised to take care of me.'

She had resorted to law, she said, in a bid to stay in the beach house which Mrs King wanted to sell. She handed over to her lawyer the tangible evidence of their closeness — joint credit cards, love letters, blank cheques which Mrs King had left for Marilyn to complete. But all that was now left for her, she said, was a life of pain. She was confined to a wheelchair after plunging 40ft from an upstairs window of the disputed home.

With her devoted husband Larry at her side, all Billie Jean could do was to wait for the court hearing which would determine whether she could evict Marilyn Barnett — and, perhaps more importantly, whether the court would find that she would have to pay her palimony for life. The hearing started in December 1981, by which time Billie Jean King was feeling the financial as much as the emotional strain. Big sports goods firms, worried that their lily-white image could be tarnished by a self-confessed gay woman, cancelled contracts with her.

The court case, when it arose, was over within two days. The judge in Los Angeles said that Marilyn's claim to live in Mrs King's beach house 'bordered on extortion' and ruled that she should be evicted. A jubilant Mrs King said afterwards: 'The case has cost me millions of dollars in lost earnings from cancelled contracts. My fans have been absolutely wonderful. One thing I know is that Marilyn is not my friend. Larry and I have lost a lot.'

Marilyn, meanwhile, said she still loved her old flame. She pledged

---

Lawrence of Arabia

The death of T. E. Lawrence was as mysterious as his life. During his heroic exploits as Lawrence of Arabia he is said to have fallen victim to perverted homosexual practices. This might explain his obsessional desire for anonimity when, after World War I, he assumed the role of 'Aircraftsman Shaw' on an RAF base in Dorset.

With the rise of fascism in Europe, Lawrence's right-wing views could have become an embarrassment. But in May 1935, on the eve of a meeting arranged with right-winger Henry Williamson, author of *Tarka The Otter*, Lawrence was speeding down a Dorset country lane on his motorcycle when he crashed trying to avoid two boys on bicycles and, according to one eyewitness, a large, black limousine.

He was taken to a military hospital and put under guard night and day. His cottage was searched. The witness who saw the black car was ordered not to mention it. No news of Lawrence's crash and his serious head injuries was released. Six days later Lawrence of Arabia died in hospital, apparently without regaining consciousness.

to keep the bundles of love letters that Billie Jean had written to her during their seven-month affair. 'I'm hostile towards Billie Jean,' she said as she left the court. 'But I'll always love her. I hope the future holds good things for both of us.'

It was another eleven months before the second part of Marilyn Barnett's claim against Billie Jean, which was for lifetime palimony, could be heard in court. That too was dismissed, and the scandal was over.

But Mrs King, determined to cock a snook at those who acted swiftly to condemn her, decided to write her autobiography, in which none of her feelings over the illicit romance were hidden. She said in the book: 'Marilyn is small and blonde, with a little bird-like voice. She struck me as nice, easily affectionate and simple. What I liked most about it was that I could escape from everything. I felt no differently with Marilyn than when I was making love with a man. My point then was, as ever: "Please, no labels." '

Movie Star Secrets

They are the dream people . . . the superstars who lend colour and fantasy to the lives of millions. In their lifetimes they are worshipped by their fans and treated with deference by those who surround them, but after their death the race is on to shatter the dream, destroy the image. And the most scandalous revelations always earn the biggest money.

Errol Flynn was accused of being a Nazi spy, a bisexual and a failure in bed.

Tyrone Power was said to have enjoyed affairs with men more than women.

Bing Crosby was portrayed as a harsh disciplinarian who drove his children to drink and nervous breakdown.

Hollywood's glamorous leading ladies — Marilyn Monroe, Jayne Mansfield, Joan Crawford, Jean Harlow and Vivien Leigh — became drink-sodden and often promiscuous bed-hoppers, according to the books that followed their deaths.

Among those who suffered the greatest blows to their reputations were the first king of comedy, Charlie Chaplin, the king of rock Elvis Presley and the 'ice queen' of Hollywood, Grace Kelly. In fact, by the early eighties, it seemed the exception rather than the rule that a star's reputation should survive intact after he or she had died and could sue no more. . . .

Some of the most astonishing of these posthumous revelations revolved around the swashbuckling character of Errol Flynn. In his lifetime he strode through Hollywood, leaving a trail of sex scandals and numerous tales of hellraising. His appetite for beautiful women was legendary, his prowess in bed unquestioned. But his image took a battering following his death in 1959.

Michael Freedland, author of the book *Errol Flynn*, alleged that one of the star's female conquests told her friends that he was poorly endowed. Another claimed that he sprinkled cocaine on his private parts to prolong lovemaking. Freedland also said that Flynn was hooked on hard drugs.

Another author, Charles Higham, claimed in his book *The Adventures of Errol Flynn* that the star was bisexual and had several homosexual affairs, including one with screen idol Tyrone Power. Higham said Flynn was terrified that his homosexuality might be discovered. It would have meant the end of his Hollywood career.

Higham wrote of Flynn and Power: 'Here were the two greatest Hollywood stars of their times, emblems of virility and masculinity, in bed together.' According to the author, the pair became lovers during a three-week Mexican holiday in 1948. Flynn went on to have other male lovers, said Higham, who claimed that his information came from the star's former secretary, Dorothy Nolan.

If Higham's sex claims were thought shocking, they were no more than mere tittle-tattle compared with what followed in a second book on the subject by the same author. In it he claimed to have proof that Flynn had been a Nazi spy during World War II.

Casting doubt on the image of patriotic heroism surrounding the star, he alleged that Flynn took photographs of US naval installations before the bombing of Pearl Harbor and passed them to Japan. Higham said Flynn also made profits from a refuelling scheme for German U-boats and had top-level Nazi contacts in the United States of America and Mexico.

Higham, who said his claims were based on secret FBI files, charged that Flynn hid a Nazi spy, Dr Hermann Erben, and used his private yacht *Sirocco* to ferry Nazis around secret coastal installations. He also claimed that Flynn was vehemently anti-British (because of his Irish blood), and was equally virulently anti-Semitic, referring to studio boss Jack Warner as 'that Jewish bastard'.

Higham's allegations about Errol Flynn 'the spy' may never be proved, but his claims about Flynn's love affair with Tyrone Power were given considerable credence by another book, *The Secret Life Of Tyrone Power*, by Hector Arce.

Arce said that the screen hero had, in his early, struggling days, accepted propositions from wealthy men in return for a meal. The writer said Power needed affairs with men throughout his life, despite the realization that if he were ever found out he would almost certainly be finished.

Power, who died in 1950, embarked on a string of widely publicized affairs with some of Hollywood's top female stars — among others, Judy Garland, Mai Zetterling, Anita Ekberg and Lana Turner. But according to Arce these liaisons were no more than a smokescreen for his homosexual activities.

A star who never hid her sexual activities — whether good, bad or downright promiscuous — was the amazingly shaped Jayne Mansfield. This top-heavy phenomenon, with an IQ said to be of genius-level 164 and with a bust measurement that almost matched, was the most outrageous character in the Hollywood of the late fifties and early sixties.

Jayne, whose career started on the New York stage, moved to Hollywood and learned that publicity could work where talent failed. She became the ultimate attention-grabber, bursting into parties in honour of rival stars and flooding the press with items of gossip. Her hair was peroxide blonde, her lips scarlet, her flaunted bosom snowy white. Everything else was pink: her Cadillac, her clothes and her Sunset Strip home, complete with heart-shaped bed, bath and swimming pool.

It all seemed pure showbiz, harmless fun . . . until soon after the night in 1967 when the car carrying her and her boyfriend, lawyer Sam Brody, hit a truck near New Orleans while the couple were travelling to a nightclub engagement. Jayne was decapitated.

The razzamatazz continued through to the funeral. And then the stories began to circulate that Jayne Mansfield had not been all she seemed. And when her daughter announced that she was writing a tell-all book, the real scandal broke. . . .

The daughter, 28-year-old Jayne Marie, branded her mother a monster. She said the sex symbol lived in a bizarre fantasy world of promiscuity, drugs, drink and devil worship.

Jayne Marie wrote the book with co-author Greg Tyler, who himself claimed to have had affairs with both mother and daughter. These were some of the amazing allegations in it.

Jayne Mansfield was said to have slept with Elvis Presley in the hope that he would sing for no fee in her film *The Girl Can't Help It*. In the morning they agreed to toss a coin to decide. Jayne lost, and Elvis gave her a pink motor-cycle as a consolation prize.

Jayne was said to have had an affair with Senator Robert Kennedy and attended beach house parties with John F. Kennedy and Peter Lawford. They would tell her daughter: 'Mommy's off to a pyjama party.'

Errol Flynn dancing with his wife-to-be, Patricia Wymore

Jayne Mansfield

She drank a bottle of bourbon a day and took huge doses of amphetamines. Tyler said he often saw her taking drugs, adding: 'Cocaine kept her going.'

She made her daughter dress like a little girl, with her breasts flattened, and forced her to crawl on the floor. The reason, according to the book, was Jayne's fear that if she were seen with a teenage daughter it would make her seem old.

Last on the list of debaucheries was the claim that Jayne held weird devil-worship ceremonies with fellow cult members in the cellar of her pink Hollywood home.

But, said Tyler, the devil worshipping got a bit crazy and Jayne ordered them out of the house. She believed that being involved in the occult had publicity value, but she finally got fed up with them. One of the mystics put a curse on her. He said she would die as a witch, either by being burned at the stake or by being decapitated — which in fact she was.

In typical Hollywood jargon, her daughter provided this epitaph for her mother: 'She may have been the Hitler of the sex symbol world as far as I'm concerned. You hated to love her and loved to hate her.'

The charges against Jayne Mansfield sounded far-fetched when they were first made by her daughter, but later the star's long-time secretary, Raymond Strait, also told of her viciousness towards the child.

Strait, another of her many lovers, said Jayne used to urge boyfriend Brody to hurt the girl. She yelled: 'Beat her! Kill her! Black her eyes! If you love me make her bleed.'

According to another writer, Martha Saxton, in her book *Jayne Mansfield And The American Fifties*, young Jayne Marie went to the police in 1967 covered with bruises and marks. She claimed she had been beaten with a leather belt at her mother's urging. No charges were brought, but the girl moved out of the family home.

Hollywood's other blonde bombshell of the period was Marilyn Monroe. Jayne Mansfield envied her and emulated her. In many ways Jayne's downfall was a parody of Marilyn's. Certainly the scandals that broke only after their deaths were a chilling parallel.

The horrifying revelations about Monroe — who died in 1962, supposedly of a drugs overdose — are chronicled in another chapter. So is the story of Elvis Presley's drug-riddled life and drug-induced death in 1977. So are tales of Charlie Chaplin's secret, scandalous sex life.

In all these cases, friends and enemies rushed into print as soon as the stars were dead. Such revelations are considered fair enough when there is no family tie between the author and the subject, but when it is a close relative who dishes the dirt on a dead idol (as in the case of Jayne Mansfield's daughter) the writer can be open to charges of betrayal.

As it transpired, Jayne Marie's story elicited much public sympathy, but that was nothing compared to the tide of compassion that greeted the publication of yet another tell-all book by the daughter of a superstar. . . .

The book was *Mommie Dearest*, an 800-page, nothing-barred biography of Joan Crawford, one of the world's best-loved stars, who died in 1977 at the age of 70. It was written by her daughter Christina, whom she adopted as an infant in 1940.

In the book Christina describes vicious beatings which her mother gave her and the three other adopted children. She would tie them to their beds if they sucked their thumbs. She would make them scrub the floors over and over again. She would have the same food served up meal after meal if any of the children failed to finish their portion.

Christina described how Crawford would come storming into the children's bedrooms in a drunken fury and smash everything in sight. How her brother Christopher ran away from home four times. And how she was sent away to school and did not see her mother for a year at a time.

She wrote graphically of her mother's alcoholic rages . . . 'Grabbing for my throat like a mad dog, with a look in her eyes that will never be erased from my memory. Her eyes were the eyes of a killer animal.'

There was, Christina said, an endless succession of 'uncles' coming to stay. After Joan Crawford married her last husband, Pepsi-Cola boss Alfred Steele, daughter Christina made the mistake of kissing her new stepfather goodnight. Her mother hit her hard, saying: 'I got my man — now you damn well go out and get your own.'

Brother Christopher also spoke venomously of their mother. He said: 'I hated the bitch. She was evil. I know that's a terrible thing to say, but it's the truth.'

Christopher, a 6ft 4in Vietnam veteran, recalled how when he was five his sister dressed him up in some of their mother's clothes. 'We were just playing but J.C. went berserk,' he said. 'She whipped me and whipped me with an army belt.'

He said his mother once taught him a lesson for playing with matches by holding his hands in the fire. His blisters took months to heal.

Another book on Crawford, by author Bob Thomas, recounted how she would invite a selection of unaccompanied males to dinner and choose one of them to stay the night.

He also detailed her drinking habits. When booking into a hotel she would give a list of the alcohol that had to be waiting for her in her room: 'Two bottles of 100 proof Smirnoff vodka, a bottle of Old Forester bourbon, a bottle of Beefeater gin and two bottles of Dom Perignon champagne.'

In the star's later years, when she was travelling the world promoting Pepsi-Cola, she claimed it was all she drank. But her innocent-looking ice-box was packed with hard liquor, and when she drank a Pepsi it was usually laced with a liberal slug of vodka. Crawford drank hard for more than 30 years, although she stopped suddenly in 1975 when she became a Christian Scientist.

Further blunt allegations were made about her in a book by Charles Castle. He claimed that the actress made a blue movie which MGM bought from a blackmailer to protect her image. He also alleged that she auditioned her leading men on the casting couch.

A clue to Joan Crawford's character and her cruel treatment of two of her adopted children is the star's own upbringing. She was the illegitimate daughter of a roving father and a poverty-stricken mother. She was put to work before she was 10, and was beaten regularly. It may explain, although not excuse, her attitude towards her own family.

After *Mommie Dearest* appeared in book form, followed by a screen adaptation starring Faye Dunaway, at least two of her family came to her defence. Her adopted twin daughters Cathy and Cindy, who grew up in the same house during much the same years, denied Christina's and Christopher's allegations.

Cathy said: 'My mother was not Mommie Dearest, as shown in the book. I have never met that person. My mother was a warm, caring human being and I will miss her all my life.'

Cindy added: 'I always knew Christina hated Mother. I understand that she had been writing that book for years. She had almost finished when Mother died. Quick as a wink she revised the thing with extra venom. In my opinion she has done an immoral thing which some day she will answer for.'

And answer for it she did. In Joan Crawford's will, two of the four children were excluded. The actress wrote: 'It is my intention to make no provision herein for my son Christopher or my daughter Christina for reasons which are well known to them.'

If Joan Crawford's promiscuous, hard-drinking ways can be partly excused by her harsh upbringing, it does nothing to explain the tragic case of Vivien Leigh. While Crawford was born the illegitimate daughter of a wastrel father and a penniless mother, Vivien Leigh was the child of a wealthy, well-connected couple, and her upper-crust stage and screen roles were a natural reflection of her real-life, genteel breeding as a young English rose.

She went on to capture the world as Scarlett O'Hara in *Gone With The Wind* and she married one of the world's greatest-ever actors, Laurence Olivier. But following her death from tuberculosis at the age of 53 in 1967, her legend was shattered by a series of grievous revelations.

Lord Olivier himself revealed that he finally left Vivien because he nearly killed her. The incident occurred one night when, mentally ill, she began slapping him with a wet flannel. He said: 'She kept striking me until I went into my room and closed the door. I could not take it any more. I came out, grabbed her and threw her across the room. She hit her head on the edge of the bed. It cut her just below the temple — an inch higher, and that would have done it. I knew then that it had ended. I was afraid of killing her.'

Olivier also recognized his wife's nymphomania and her one-night stands with low-class pick-ups. But her most tempestuous affair was with actor Peter Finch. Once at a Hollywood reception she drunkenly tried to stab Finch's first wife Tamara with a pair of scissors. She was sedated and later sent back to England.

The affair ended after two years with a confrontation between Olivier and Finch at the Oliviers' country home in Oxfordshire. After dinner the two men went into the library to try to resolve the triangle. Suddenly Vivien threw open the doors and said: 'Will one of you come to bed with me now?' Finch left the house and promised never to see the actress again.

Just as Vivien Leigh's 'perfect' background failed to save her from self-destruction, so 30 years earlier another brilliant career ended with the premature death of Jean Harlow, only child of a well-to-do middle-class dentist in Kansas City. But sadly for Jean — real name Helen Carpentier — it was not her loving father who became her dominating influence but, following a remarriage, her grasping, greedy, sex-mad stepfather.

Harlow, the first real sex goddess of the 'talkies', set a style of raw sensuality that broke the mould of previous, simpering leading ladies. Yet under the unhealthy influence of her mother, Jean Harlow Carpentier, and her Svengali-like stepfather, Marino Bello, she appeared to be incapable of sustaining a romantic relationship of her own.

She eloped from school at the age of 16 to wed a 21-year-old boyfriend, but the marriage lasted just one night and the bridegroom's family had it annulled. After that episode, serious boyfriends were few and far between for the blossoming teenager. It was later rumoured that her secret lover was her own stepfather.

When the family moved to Los Angeles, the kid from Kansas helped pay their rent by taking bit-parts in films. She appeared in a Laurel and Hardy film, and Stan Laurel pointed her out to agent Arthur Landau, who was to become a lifelong friend. Howard Hughes signed her up and made her a star in the movie *Hell's Angels*. MGM bought her up, and studio boss Louis B. Mayer lauded her as representing 'normal sex, real sex, beautiful sex — the pure sex that is common to the people of America'.

However, although her fans never knew it until after her death, 'normal sex' was not one of the things Jean Harlow was about to enjoy.

In 1932 the 21-year-old star married a 40-year-old MGM film producer named Paul Bern, a quiet, sensitive man who, unlike her stepfather, had provided a fund of good advice in the furtherance of Jean's career.

Bern took his bride home for a wedding night which proved a disaster, and two months later he was dead — shot with a bullet through the head. He left this suicide note:

Dearest Dear — Unfortunately this is the only way to make good the frightful wrong I have done you and to wipe out my frightful humiliation. I love you — Paul.

He added a mysterious postscript:

You understand that last night was only a comedy.

Despite the worldwide banner headlines and the press speculation about the shattering scandal, Jean steadfastly refused to explain the meaning of Bern's note and the events that had led to his suicide. It took the actress's own untimely death five years later to bring the full story out into the open.

According to her agent Arthur Landau, Jean had received a terrible shock on her wedding night when she discovered that her new husband was extraordinarily under-endowed, and was probably impotent. She may have laughed at his sexual inadequacy, or he may have been ashamed at his own attempts at lovemaking, but the result was a beating for Jean.

The following morning Jean telephoned Landau and asked him for help. He drove to Bern's house, found the producer sleeping naked on the floor and removed Jean to his own home. There she revealed that her husband had beaten her with a cane until it broke, and had then hit her and bitten her on her legs and thighs. The fury of the attack sickened Landau, but after treatment by a doctor, Jean begged to be returned to the marital home, where the following day the beaming couple posed for formal wedding photographs at their VIP reception.

The beating resulted in liver damage from which Jean never fully recovered. Yet the couple continued to play out an elaborate charade in public . . . until the night of 4 September. That was when Bern, who had banked on the screen goddess being able to cure his sexual problems, finally acknowledged his failure. He arrived in the marital bedroom that night in a contraption designed to make the most of his meagre assets. His wife was disgusted. The following day Paul Bern put a gun to his head.

Jean Harlow's reaction was not the usual one of a grieving widow. She embarked on a prolonged sex-and-booze binge, first in Los Angeles and then in San Francisco, in the course of which she cut off her famous platinum blonde tresses. When she returned to Hollywood, Louis B. Mayer, who had only recently recovered his calm after the anguish of explaining away Bern's suicide note, ordered the studio wigmaker to repair the damage to his superstar's crowning asset.

Mayer's patience finally ran out when Jean eloped to marry her third husband, 38-year-old film cameraman Harold Losson. The studio suspended her for a month. The marriage lasted eight.

Jean Harlow's next serious romance was reputed to have been with actor William Powell. But it never came to fruition. In 1937 she fell seriously ill with a gall bladder infection and on 7 June she died. At her funeral Nelson Eddy sang *Ah Sweet Mystery Of Life*.

Two of the best-loved stars Hollywood has ever produced were Bing Crosby and Grace Kelly. Hearts melted when they sang *True Love* together in the immortal musical *High Society*. And no one could think ill of them in real life. But soon after Bing collapsed and died on a Mediterranean golf course some less than flattering epitaphs began to appear. The same happened when Grace Kelly — by then Princess Grace of Monaco — died in a car crash in her principality.

Old Groaner Bing's lovable *White Christmas* image took its severest knock from one of his four sons by his first wife, Dixie. The son, Gary, who was 43 when the star died in 1977, painted a picture of a cold, cruel father. In his book *Bing's Boy* he said his father beat him and his brothers with a leather belt and humiliated him by calling him 'stupid' and 'fatso'.

Gary blamed Bing for his alcoholism (since cured), and for youngest brother Lindsay's nervous breakdown. Friends were seldom invited to the Crosby home, said Gary, because Bing did not want them to see what he was really like with his family.

More tales of Bing the heartless father came from Mrs Eve Kelly, a nanny to his three eldest sons. She said: 'All they wanted from their father was love but they never got it. He tried to drill into me that I should punish the children on Wednesdays for all the things they had done wrong during the week. But I couldn't do that. It didn't seem fair.'

Even one of Bing's closest friends, his authorized biographer Charles

---

D. H. Lawrence

D. H. Lawrence's last novel, *Lady Chatterley's Lover*, provided the literary trial of the century when its publishers were prosecuted in 1960 under the Obscene Publications Act. The book — previously available only under the counter in Britain — chronicled the passionate love affair between an aristocrat and her gamekeeper. In writing the book, Lawrence had said his aim was to make the 'sex relation valid and precious instead of shameful'. The prosecution claimed that passages in the novel were obscene. After a much-publicized trial, the jury sided with Lawrence and the book that had been labelled scandalous and immoral became freely available. The law was made to look an ass.

Thompson, revealed some unsavoury home truths. He said Bing's second marriage, to Kathryn, was always stormy and was on the verge of breaking up when he died. He also told of the wealthy singer's penny-pinching meanness and his coldness towards his children, whom he often caned.

Thompson said: 'Gary was once woken up at dawn by his father ripping the bedclothes from him and shouting "Get out of this house — you are nothing but a troublemaker." '

'Bing once told me, "Maybe I didn't lay into them with a belt as often as I should have done." '

Allegations made about Princess Grace after her death were even more astonishing. Author Sarah Bradford claimed that the ex-actress's image as the 'ice queen' of Hollywood was a cover-up for her scandalous sex life. Before quitting America to marry Prince Rainier of Monaco, she had a series of illicit affairs which were hushed up.

Ray Milland, who met Grace when they filmed *Dial M For Murder*, was 'gaga over her', according to Sarah's book *Princess Grace*. But she 'dropped Ray like a hot potato' when his wife threatened divorce. The book also alleged that Grace had 'a physical affair' with Clark Gable.

Of course, such scandalous allegations can only be made when a star is no longer around to answer back — and to sue.

Errol Flynn

Errol Flynn hit the front pages in 1942 with the headline: 'Star On Double Rape Charge.' The alleged offences were 'statutory rape', the Californian legal term for sex with a minor.

The trial became a farce. Nightclub dancer Peggy Larne Satterlee went to court in pigtails and bobbysocks to describe Flynn's improper advances. But she failed to convince the court that she was under 18, and Flynn, who admitted having seduced her, was acquitted.

Then a 17-year-old shop assistant told the court how Flynn had undressed her and climbed into bed with only his boots on.

Again he was acquitted. But he had broken Hollywood's golden rule 'Thou shalt not get caught', and he did not find work again for nearly a year.

In 1978 Flynn's amazing former sex palace was put up for sale at $2 million. The bedrooms were fitted with two-way mirrors and microphones for the entertainment of Flynn and his guests at his bawdy parties. They would look and listen as couples paired off and made love. A real-estate agent said: 'The orgies that went on here would make Hollywood today look like a Sunday school.'

Princess Michael of Kent

For a member of Britain's royal family, even if only by marriage, the life of Princess Michael of Kent has been a strange one.

Born Marie-Christine von Reibnitz in Czechoslovakia in January 1945, she was told childhood stories of her father piling their possessions on a handcart to join refugees fleeing before the advancing Russian armies. The family settled in Vienna, but when Marie-Christine was just a year old her parents split up. Her father went to Mozambique to become a citrus farmer on an inherited estate. Her mother, the Countess Marianne, continued to live with her daughter and young son in Vienna until in 1950 they emigrated to Australia.

They settled in Waverley, on the southern shores of Sydney Harbour, where Marianne trained as a hairdresser and eventually ran her own salon. Her daughter became a weekly boarder at Kincoppall Convent school in nearby Elizabeth Bay. There she was looked on as athletic, artistic and, by virtue of her background, a bit of a mystery.

When Marie-Christine finished school she spent a year with her father in Mozambique before touring Europe studying the history of art. She returned to Sydney to do a course in shorthand and typing before moving to England to learn interior decorating — and to start a new life of her own in the London of the 'swinging sixties'.

She met Tom Troubridge, an Old Etonian merchant banker, and in 1971, when she was aged 26, they married. The marriage lasted no more than two years before a discreet separation was arranged. Marie-Christine moved into a modest house in Chelsea and rejoined the social merry-go-round. At a party she found herself sitting next to Prince Michael of Kent, then a captain in the Royal Hussars.

They began going out together. It was not serious at first, but it soon developed into love. The royal family were reported to be disturbed — Marie-Christine, it was argued, was a Roman Catholic, whereas Michael was a Protestant. And she had a broken marriage behind her.

The marriage, on 30 June 1978, was a compromise. They were wed in a civil ceremony in Vienna's town hall. Neither the Queen nor Prince Philip attended. Among the guests were Princess Anne, the Duke of Kent, Princess Alexandra, her husband Angus Ogilvy, Lady Helen Windsor, Lord Louis Mountbatten (who had proved a great support in their romance) and the bride's father, Baron von Reibnitz.

Even that simple ceremony had been touch-and-go. The couple had planned to marry at the ancient Schottenkirche, the Scottish abbey church in Vienna, on 1 July. But only two days before the ceremony they received the news that the Pope had refused to annul Marie-Christine's marriage to Troubridge and grant a dispensation for the royal wedding. So, as the guests flew in, the bride sadly left her silk wedding gown in her hotel wardrobe and married the prince in a simple suit at the civil ceremony. Only on the following day was she able to wear her bridal gown for the official photographs after taking communion at church.

The couple returned to live in royal apartments at Kensington Palace. They also bought a country home in Gloucestershire. Michael left the army to take up directorships in the City of London. A son was born a year after the marriage, and a daughter 18 months later. The only note of personal sadness was the news that the princess's father had died at his home in Mozambique at the age of 89.

Despite the happiness of her marriage, the life of the glamorous blonde royal 'newcomer' was blighted by controversy.

Despite her hard work boosting the image of royalty, she remained the outsider of her husband's family. Newspaper columns were filled with gleeful reports on the royal family's supposed attitude to the new member in their midst. The Queen was reputed to call her 'Our Val' — a reference to her Valkyrie-like looks and manner. 'She's far too grand for the likes of us,' the Queen is reported to have said of her tartly. Viscount Linley, the Queen's nephew, was once asked what he would give his worst enemy; his reported reply was: 'Dinner with Princess Michael.'

The more the princess tried to become one of the 'real royals', the more she gained a reputation as 'Princess Pushy'. She worked harder than many of her husband's relatives. The public loved her. But the more she tried, the further away acceptance seemed to be.

And all the while a time bomb was ticking away which would shame her own family and shake her husband's. . . .

It exploded on 15 April 1985 when a reporter from the London *Daily Mirror* telephoned Buckingham Palace and asked if it were true that Princess Michael's father, far from being a victim of the war, had in fact been a major in Adolf Hitler's feared, brutal SS.

The palace press office left a note for the princess in her apartment at Kensington Palace — and at six o'clock on that Monday evening she returned home after a busy day, opened the letter and learned the awful truth.

According to the *Mirror*'s chief royal-watcher, James Whitaker, the 40-year-old princess at first panicked. She said she would do anything to prevent publication of such a 'wicked lie'. As she talked of writs and injunctions, her aides tried to calm her. They advised her to check every fact before reacting.

Princess Michael telephoned her mother in Sydney, and as she listened to the old lady's hesitant answers she realized that the terrible truth would have to be told. The Queen's press secretary, Michael Shea, was called in, and after 100 long minutes of agonizing, the princess agreed to an official statement. It read:

Princess Michael confirmed tonight that it is true that her father was a member of the SS. It came as a total surprise to her when she heard the news from James Whitaker. And it came as a total shock.

There will be no further comment or statement from the princess.

Worldwide reaction was immediate. The scandal made the front pages of papers throughout North America, Europe and Australasia. British and European members of parliament demanded an inquiry. Leading American Jews condemned the 'royal cover-up'. And as the storm grew, the full details of her father's involvement with the Nazis was revealed.

Ironically, the facts about Baron Gunther von Reibnitz had been publicly available for years. They were to be found in dusty archives just three miles from Buckingham Palace — in official lists of senior SS officers which have been held at the Imperial War Museum since the early sixties. The records showed that von Reibnitz, born on 8 September 1894, was an Unterstürmführer — equivalent to the rank of a British second-lieutenant — in 1935. By the last entry, in October 1944, he had risen to Sturmbannführer, the equivalent of major. The lists showed that he won an Iron Cross (second class) and a Front Line Soldiers Cross in World War I. Another honour bestowed on him was the SS 'death's head' ring.

The bald facts to be gleaned from the war museum files masked a depth of embarrassing information about the Nazi major's military and political connections. His Nazi party number, 412855, revealed the early stage at which he espoused their evil cause. According to Nazi-hunter Simon Wiesenthal: 'This means that he pledged his loyalty to Hitler and to the Hitler ideals and hatreds in the early 1920s.'

In an SS questionnaire, asking permission from the Führer to marry the countess — the second of his four wives — he said: 'I was used as a political speaker in the years of the struggle.'

But according to the *Mirror*, which broke the story, his Nazi role before joining the SS in 1933 at the age of 39 was much more active. The newspaper even suggested that he may have been planted as a Hitler spy in the Nazi street-fighting storm troopers, the SA. He switched to the SS shortly before Hitler wiped out the SA and was promoted four days after the bloodbath. According to the *Mirror*, he acted as 'the eyes and ears of Hermann Goering', the Führer's right-hand man. His reward was Goering's personal recommendation for one of his army postings.

As a captain, von Reibnitz first saw action in September 1939 on the Polish plains. He boasted about having fought battles at Pless

Nikolai and Przesna Rusks, although no major fighting was recorded in these areas.

The truth is more likely to be that he did a desk job well behind the front lines and was removed from active service to spend most of the war in Silesia, as 'personally requested by Goering', according to the *Mirror*.

In 1944 the baron decided to rejoin the Roman Catholic Church, which he had deserted years earlier. His immediate superiors judged this a 'character weakness' and he resigned from the SS.

Simon Wiesenthal, questioned when news of the baron's SS involvement broke, said that von Reibnitz was not a wanted man. 'He did not, as far as any of our records show, take part in any atrocities.' But the SS under their dreaded leader Heinrich Himmler, were in charge of all concentration camps. And even if he were not personally involved, observers pointed out that the baron would have mixed with those who did, and must have known of their activities.

The SS was divided into three branches — the front-line Waffen (or 'Armed') SS, responsible for massacring entire populations such as at Lidice in Poland; the Leibstandarte, which provided a bodyguard for Hitler and other top Nazis; and the Allegemeine, the general branch which included the 'death's head' brigade of concentration camp guards. Himmler controlled all three, and members were regularly moved from one section to another.

As an SS officer, the baron was automatically listed as being part of Hitler's racial experiment, the Lebensborn programme, designed to produce a 'master race'. He was expected to produce strong, healthy children of good Aryan stock.

The fact that his most successful child, Marie-Christine, became labelled by the Queen as 'Our Val' because of her blue-eyed, blonde, Aryan, Valkyrie-like looks is an ironic footnote to the revelations that were to shake her and the royal family four decades later.

Despite Princess Michael's initial vow that she would make 'no further comment or statement', allegations of a cover-up grew so strong that she felt obliged to go on nationwide television in an attempt to end the controversy. Looking strained, she said that although she knew her father had been a Nazi party member, she had never been aware that he had been in the SS.

'It is a deep shame for me,' she said. 'I think it was sufficiently shocking that he had been in the Nazi party but I did not think to look further. It came as a very great blow to me because I always rather hero-worshipped him.

'When told this report was coming out in the *Daily Mirror*, I immediately telephoned my mother and said: "Guess what they are trying to pin on me now." And she said: "But I'm afraid it is true."

'I have been in a sort of state of shell-shock ever since. But it is

---

Tom Keating

The art scandal of the century was brought to light by what forger Tom Keating described as his 'Sexton Blakes' — cockney rhyming slang for fakes. Keating, a former naval stoker, went on trial at the Old Bailey in 1979 when he was 62 and many reputations in the art world were ruined by the evidence he gave against 'greedy' dealers. By Keating's own, rough count, no fewer than 2,500 of his fake pictures were hanging in galleries or on collectors' walls. The forger said he could no longer remember most of the forgeries he had turned out — so no one would ever know which of the world's 'old masters' were fake and which were genuine. Keating himself escaped any court penalty; charges against him were dropped when his health deteriorated.

---

something I'll have to come to terms with, and I know that I shall. I don't like it but I have to live with it.'

The princess then talked of a 'document which actually exonerates my father — which states quite clearly that his position with the SS was an honorary one'. She added: 'I was brought up to believe that the SS meant one thing — concentration camps for Jews and so on. I have now discovered that he was not involved in anything like that at all.' But far from ending the controversy, Princess Michael's television statement only added fuel to the blazing row over her father.

Simon Wiesenthal dismissed as 'absolutely unbelievable' her claim that her father was merely an honorary member of the SS who never wore its uniform. He was one of the first people to join the SS in 1933, and it was 'impossible to think he never wore the uniform'. He added: 'That may be what her father told her but it's not the truth.'

Australian author Barry Everingham, who was writing a book about the princess at the time the scandal broke, claimed that the baron's SS involvement was well known in royal and political circles. 'The Queen was warned, the Prime Minister was warned and Prince Michael was warned,' he said.

Few observers doubted that Princess Michael had been secretly 'vetted' before her marriage — either by Scotland Yard or MI5 and probably involving the expertise of royal publishers Debretts. Hugh Peskett, chief researcher at Debretts, said: 'People on the inside must have known; I was told about it in confidence.' And Debretts publishing director Harold Brooks-Baker commented: 'I did not know this was a secret. I have heard it mentioned many times.'

Meanwhile, newspapers rushed out new revelations about Princess Michael — in particular, questioning her close friendship with an American millionaire. It was also said that when the teenaged Marie-Christine visited her father in Mozambique, she regularly met and dined with his closest friends — fellow SS officers who had fled to the Portuguese colony after the war. Baron von Reibnitz was said to have been revered by the other Nazis, and to have had a reputation as a harsh employer of his African labour force.

It was also claimed that Princess Michael had spoken to close friends about her family's past at least six months before her marriage into the royal family. She was said to have been extremely worried about whether she and Prince Michael would be given the Queen's permission to wed.

In the race to produce Nazi links with the royal family, it was also revealed that the Queen's own husband was related to an SS man. Documents in London's Imperial War Museum showed that Prince Philip's German brother-in-law, Prince Christoph of Hesse, had been a brigadier-general in Hitler's élite corps. He married Philip's sister, Sophie, in 1930 and was killed in action in 1943.

Princess Michael tried to counter the growing storm by instituting an urgent search for documents that would help clear her father's name. With the help of the British ambassador in Bonn, Sir Julian Bullard, they were found in Germany within the week.

The documents were the findings of a tribunal held in Upper Bavaria in 1948. Baron von Reibnitz had gone to the tribunal to appeal against a lower court ruling under the post-war 'de-Nazification' programme. This court had failed to clear the baron and instead had placed him under the category of 'less incriminated person' because of his SS activities.

Von Reibnitz was not happy with the decision and took his case to the appeal tribunal, which agreed with him and set the earlier verdict aside.

The tribunal found that the baron had joined the Nazi party in 1931 'in the belief that National Socialism would bring about economic recovery'. He obtained his SS ranks as an honorary title through his post as chief ranger in charge of hunting in his part of Germany. He had the right to wear his SS uniform but not to give orders. In 1944 he was dismissed from the SS because of conflicts with his immediate superiors.

After further incurring the displeasure of the party by becoming a Roman Catholic, he was threatened with a posting to a *dirlewanger* punishment battalion. He used his social influence and his position in the German regular army to avoid this fate.

The tribunal's judgment stated:

The evidence has not adduced references to the effect that the accused should be regarded as a militarist or as having reaped any benefit. He was to be regarded as falling within the category of nominal party member since he took only a nominal part in National Socialism and lent it only insignificant support. The accused was not a member of any organization condemned as criminal in the Nuremberg judgments.

The tribunal said that the baron was 'equivalent to a non-accused person'. But they rejected his petition seeking total exoneration.

The documents were enough to quell the scandal. Newspapers, which a week earlier had been printing headlines such as 'This Bloody Disgrace', fell silent. And the princess herself was again able to open a paper without fearing the worst.

The strain, however, was evident. Making a speech at an official function, she spoke hesitatingly of her ordeal . . . then her voice broke and she was reduced to tears.

Public affection swung to her. At one event she attended she was cheered louder than the Queen. The girl from Sydney was back on top. The princess seemed to have survived the storm.

Margaret Trudeau

As wife of the Canadian prime minister, Margaret Trudeau had an unlimited capacity for creating sensational headlines. Her husband Pierre's ruling Liberal Party was scandalized by her tales of pot-smoking, her four-letter words, her reported attempt to lure Britain's Prince Charles to Paris and finally her amazingly ill-timed kiss-and-tell autobiography just one month before a general election.

Margaret first met Trudeau, a swinging, eligible bachelor 29 years her senior, in Tahiti during the flower-power era. Years later she said she was and still remained a 'flower child'. Her holiday was being paid for by her father, James Sinclair, a wealthy former Canadian Cabinet minister.

She married Trudeau in 1971, and it soon became clear that the debonair Canadian leader was in for some embarrassing moments.

But the incident that shocked his countrymen most — and, it was said, marked the beginning of the end for their marriage — was her much-publicized weekend with the Rolling Stones rock group in 1977.

Margaret, who had embarked on a career as a 'photo-journalist', travelled to Toronto to watch the group recording in concert at a rock pub, leaving Pierre babysitting 240 miles away in Ottawa. Wearing a tight-fitting blue boiler suit, she danced to the band's music, took photographs of the Stones and sat at the feet of Mick Jagger as he sang.

'It's quite a buzz,' she told friends. And when the Stones gave a repeat concert the following night the premier's wife was there again. She spent the night in the same hotel as the Stones, in the room next

Mrs Margaret Trudeau

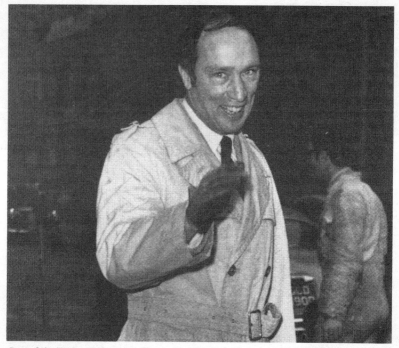

Canada's Prime Minister, Pierre Trudeau during a visit to London

to Keith Richard (who had just been charged in Canada with drug offences).

Pop music writer Lisa Robinson, who was with the Stones in Toronto over the weekend, said Margaret was seen 'wandering around hotel corridors dressed in a white bathrobe and hanging out with the band'. As Miss Robinson watched her pose for photographs with the group, drummer Charlie Watts was heard to mutter: 'I wouldn't want my wife associating with us.'

On both nights Margaret arrived for the concerts in a limousine with Mick Jagger. She said: 'I've always loved the Stones. I've always wanted to take their pictures and now I've got the chance.'

After leaving the second concert at 1 a.m. on Sunday, Margaret was driven off in an estate car, sitting beside Mick Jagger and Keith Richard. They went to a party which lasted until 7 a.m.

Then, to the further horror of her husband's political supporters, Margaret followed the Stones to New York. There one of the city's leading gossip writers, Suzy on the *Daily News*, wrote about the friendship between Mrs Trudeau and the Stones' spiky-haired guitarist Ron

Wood. She said: 'Ron is her very special Stone — and you can roll with that one. Ron is at the Plaza Hotel in New York. He can probably tell you more about where Margaret is staying than maybe anyone else.'

Margaret was absolutely furious. Canadian government ministers blanched. The Canadian dollar lost 1½ cents.

Even the Stones appeared to have become embarrassed by the publicity. Their spokesman Paul Wasserman said: 'The last thing in the world the Stones want is any scandal, any crazies. Their whole energy is needed for new albums. Jagger and the others are in New York for specific things. Mrs Trudeau and the group have completely different interests in New York.'

Jagger was exaggeratedly off-hand about the affair. He said: 'We just had a passing acquaintance for two nights. She just wanted to be introduced. Princess Margaret wanted to be introduced in London; Lee Radziwill followed us. These ladies are very charming to have around. There is no suggestion of anything more.'

Meanwhile the Toronto newspapers were thundering: 'Someone should control the lady. It is unacceptable for the wife of the prime minister to be cavorting with a group like the Rolling Stones. Most of them have, at one time or another, been involved with drugs.'

Margaret's response was that she did not wish to be 'a rose in my husband's lapel'.

Pierre Trudeau, then preparing for an official visit by British prime minister James Callaghan and foreign secretary David Owen and their wives, implored Margaret to return home from New York, where she was now staying with her friend Princess Yasmin Khan, daughter of Rita Hayworth and Aly Khan.

But Margaret was reported as saying: 'I've had enough. After six years I abdicate. I no longer want to be in an official capacity. If people cannot see what kind of life I've had for the past six years and why I choose not to live it any more, then I'm sorry. I'm just not going to devote my time to that any more. That may be selfish but I think everyone has the right to be selfish sometimes. And the pressure to do certain things that you don't find pleasant — certain things that you find boring or downright insulting to your integrity — is really too much.'

Whether or not she found 'boring' the prospect of greeting her husband's British guests and being hostess at a banquet for them, Margaret Trudeau was eventually persuaded to return home, just in time for the arrival of the Callaghans and the Owens. She arrived at Ottawa airport wearing dark glasses and accompanied by a woman friend. She was whisked away in a limousine. The next day, however, she refused to host a lunch for Mrs Callaghan and Mrs Owen while their husbands talked elsewhere.

Trudeau and his wife had a blazing row, throwing things at one another, and two days later Margaret was frankly explaining her black eye. 'Pierre said I deserved a good spanking and belted me,' she said. 'But that night we made love and it was one of the most exciting times we have ever had together. It was wonderful, I don't think it had ever been so good before.'

Seven weeks later, however, the couple separated officially. They made the decision at a 35-minute meeting at Ottawa airport, where their paths happened to cross. Pierre had custody of the children — Justin, aged five, Sacha, four, and Michel, one.

A terse announcement from Trudeau's office said: 'Pierre accepts Margaret's decision with regret and both pray that their separation will lead to a better relationship between themselves.' Margaret confirmed that she was going to find an apartment in New York. 'In future I will be known as Margaret Sinclair, freelance photographer,' she said.

Although the couple later reunited, the self-inflicted blows to their marriage proved too strong. Margaret pursued her photography, then turned actress for two films, neither of which made an amazing impact. She wrote a book, *Beyond Reason*, which was seen by many as a public confession of her misdeeds. Her name was linked by gossip columnists with King Hussein, Ryan O'Neal, Senator Edward Kennedy and mineral-water boss Bruce Nevins. But it is for her often-innocent *faux pas* that Margaret Trudeau remains best remembered. . . .

There was the time when she attended a formal Washington dinner wearing a too-mini skirt, and with a run in her stocking. Or the time at a state banquet in Caracas, Venezuela, when she embarrassed the guests by singing an uninspired composition of her own in praise of the president's wife. Or when, during an election campaign, she wandered unwashed and barefoot into a Vancouver hotel in the middle of the night and asked for her husband's suite.

To staid Canadians, the astonishment at some of her deeds was compounded by her readiness to talk about them. She even embarrassed the British royal family. . . .

She once attempted to get an interview with Princess Margaret by barging up to her at a New York lunch and, while she was still eating, demanding a chat. It was frostily indicated that she should go away.

On another occasion she was reported to have attempted to lure Prince Charles to visit her in Paris. She is said to have told friends: 'When I first met him in Ottawa I knew I'd got him interested. He deliberately peeked down my blouse. I rarely wear a bra and, since the blouse buttons were undone, he told me I was pretty enough to be an actress.'

When some time later she was in Paris on a photographic assignment, Margaret tried to persuade the prince to meet her. She telephoned him on his private direct line at Buckingham Palace, and was told he would ring her back. A palace operator later rang her Paris hotel saying: 'Prince Charles is telephoning for Mrs Trudeau.' Unfortunately for her, Margaret had booked in under her maiden name, Sinclair, and the hotel failed to put through the call. Margaret was furious.

But not half as furious as Canada's Liberal Party bigwigs at some of Mrs Trudeau's more amazing revelations.

Never the diplomat, she was once asked about reports that she had smoked pot. She replied: 'Of course I smoked marijuana, in Morocco. But the world of hard drugs is foreign to me.' Then, as if thinking her remarks were not quite up to the usual shock factor, she added: 'I still smoke marijuana from time to time.'

Prime ministers' wives — or even ex-prime ministers' ex-wives — are not expected to say things like that. But that is a lesson that Margaret Trudeau delighted in never having learned.

Watergate

Nightwatchman Frank Wills was only mildly annoyed when he tugged at the 'locked' door in the basement garage of the Watergate office block, and it swung open freely. In the beam of his powerful flashlight the cause was soon obvious. A piece of adhesive tape had been stretched tightly across the latch. Wills peeled the tape from the lock and stepped from the garage into the darkened corridor leading to the offices.

Nothing stirred.

There wasn't anything sinister about the tape holding the door unlocked, he decided. From the inside of the office block, a simple turn of a handle opened the door. In an emergency like a fire, anyone inside the building could escape quickly through the door into the garage. Anyone trying to enter the Watergate offices from the outside, though, needed a key to unlock the door.

There was a simple explanation for the tape, Wills reasoned. A maintenance cleaner struggling with heavy equipment between the corridor and his parked car, who didn't have his hands free to reach his key, could have taped the door open for convenience.

Just to reassure himself, Wills checked the corridor once more. The office doors were firmly locked; everything was in darkness.

It was 12.45 a.m. and time for Wills to take a break. Satisfied that he had blocked the minor breach in security, the nightwatchman strolled across the street to have a coffee in the all-night restaurant of a nearby hotel.

An hour later Wills was back on duty. He reached for his own bunch of keys to let himself in through the garage door to the office block. Again the door swung open freely. A fresh strip of tape had been spread across the lock.

This wasn't the work of a maintenance man. And the culprit was probably still inside. From the emergency phone in the basement Wills called the Washington Police. Three plainclothes officers in an unmarked car responded within minutes.

The police crept along the corridor until they reached the door leading to the stairwell. That too was taped open, and so was every door leading up to the sixth floor. With their revolvers cocked, they walked warily into the sixth-floor offices. Seeing a figure crouching behind a desk, one policeman warned sternly: 'Come out . . . and keep your hands in the air.'

To their amazement not just one man raised his arms. Four others stepped out from behind partitions and filing cabinets and surrendered quietly. In a token attempt to delay the discovery of their true identities, the men gave false names to the police. But it was immediately obvious they were not just sneak-thieves.

They had been caught red-handed with a variety of spy cameras, bugging equipment, disguises and thousands of dollars in new dollar bills. In one of the notebooks found on the burglars was a direct-line telephone number to the White House.

The following day, 18 June 1972, newspapers carried some brief reports about the break-in at the offices of the Democratic Party in the Watergate office complex on the banks of the Potomac River in Washington, District of Columbia.

A thousand miles away in Florida, where he was basking in the sunshine of a brief holiday, President Richard Nixon read the reports with little more than passing interest.

'A third-rate burglary,' he mused to an aide. 'I wonder what's behind it?'

A few hundred yards away from the White House in Washington, at the offices of Nixon's own Republican election campaign headquarters, Robert Odle, the head of administration for the Citizens' Committee to Re-Elect the President, had heard the news of the break-in and couldn't hide his amusement and relief.

'It couldn't happen to our office,' he boasted smiling to a secretary. 'We've got an old CIA hand in charge of our security; he's a real professional. His name is Jim McCord.'

At around the same time James W. McCord, former senior officer in the Central Intelligence Agency, was appearing in Superior Court being charged with burglary. With him in the dock were Frank Sturgis, a veteran US Marine turned soldier of fortune; Bernard Barker, born of American parents in Cuba; and Virgilio Gonzalez and Eugenio Martinez, both Cuban exiles living in the United States and both former agents for the CIA.

All five men had been hired by officials inside the White House and the Citizens' Committee to Re-Elect the President, known to friends and foes alike as CREEP. Their mission had been to burgle the files of President Nixon's political rivals, to spy on them, to harass them and to invent scandals to discredit them. Criminal acts of burglary and bribery were just part of their stock in trade.

On orders from CREEP and the White House, they were being directed to commit criminal acts and to undermine American democracy to ensure at all costs that Richard Nixon was re-elected in 1972 for a second four-year term in the White House. To achieve their ends CREEP had more than $30 million at its disposal.

After the arrest of the five burglars at Watergate, the top priority for CREEP was to try to cover up their involvement, to deny any connections between themselves and the criminals. And the senior staff members of Nixon's own team at the White House had to make sure the President himself was not linked with them.

At first they succeeded. In the six months between the Watergate break-in and the presidential election, the connection between this flagrant law-breaking and the White House was hushed up in a conspiracy of silence and perjury. President Nixon was duly re-elected. Nothing, it seemed, could prevent him from achieving his raw political ambition of keeping the power of the White House in his grasp. And then the cover-up began to fall apart.

In the period between the break-in and the election, FBI agents investigating the crimes had only uncovered firm evidence against two low-ranking White House officials, E. Howard Hunt and G. Gordon Liddy, to implicate them in the planning and execution of the Watergate burglary.

Hunt, an outwardly modest and unassuming man, was a former CIA agent who had a creditable wartime record of working behind Japanese enemy lines, and who had acted as a liaison officer with Cuban exiles trying to overthrow the regime of Fidel Castro. By the late sixties, Hunt was beginning to feel that life was passing him by. He had been spending most of his time dashing off spy novels and paperback thrillers and brooding on the 'menace of communism'. He was delighted to receive the call to join the White House staff in 1971.

Gordon Liddy was a flamboyant ex-army officer who had become a law graduate and assistant district attorney, a fiery anti-communist who tried to win the Republican nomination as a congressional candidate in New York. There he shocked his potential voters by taking his jacket off on the election platform and displaying a shoulder holster

White House officials: John D Ehrlichman (left), Henry Peterson (right)

complete with loaded pistol. He had been working as a government drugs investigator when he and Hunt were invited to form President Nixon's secret Special Investigations Unit.

In the web of paranoia which Nixon wove around himself, the spy-turned-fiction-writer and the uncontrollable narcotics agent were two eager predatory spiders.

They tackled their first assignment with gusto.

In June 1971 the *New York Times* had begun to publish a series of secret archive papers detailing the unsavoury aspects of covert American military activity in Vietnam. Nixon was beside himself with fury. His wildly irrational reaction and demands for revenge conditioned the White House staff to stop at nothing to satisfy his urge to destroy his opponents by fair means or foul.

A former government official, Daniel Ellsberg, was suspected of leaking the documents. And the job of Special Investigations — nicknamed the 'Plumbers' — was to plug the leaks.

The White House had asked the CIA for a report on Ellsberg, claiming he might have committed treason. The CIA response didn't please Nixon. The agency considered that Ellsberg had not been traitorous but had acted out of a misguided sense of patriotism.

The White House wanted to conduct its own investigation, and 'Plumbers' Hunt and Liddy were ordered to obtain information from the files of a Los Angeles psychiatrist who had been treating Ellsberg. Their approach was direct. Posing as doctors, the two men talked their way into the psychiatrist's office when he was absent and photographed the security arrangements of doors and filing cabinets.

A week later they returned with a team of three 'burglars', including two of the Cubans later arrested at the Watergate building. While Hunt and Liddy watched discreetly from a distance, the Cubans broke into the office and ransacked the files. The burglary provided little of use, but it gave Hunt and Liddy the taste for breaking and entering.

The 'Plumbers' continued to be kept busy. The President's senior aides and legal advisers wanted information and gossip about the targets for the White House's latest hate campaign: the 'Enemies List'.

The object of the list, the President's legal counsel John Dean explained in a secret memo to staff, was to compile a register of prominent Americans who were critical of the President and to persecute them and deprive them of their rights.

All the departments of the US government bureaucracy would be used against the President's so-called 'enemies'.

Businessmen would fail to qualify for government contracts or grants. Individuals would be ground down by constant litigation and threats of prosecution. The Internal Revenue would sift through their tax returns to penalize them if possible.

Any important personality who did not wholeheartedly support Richard Nixon could be subject to the White House vendetta. The 'Enemies List' included 200 individuals and 18 organizations. They ranged from former ambassadors to industrialists, lawyers and academics. In the four-inch-thick file were the names of 57 journalists who were targets for FBI taps on their telephones and a dozen internationally known entertainers, including Paul Newman, Jane Fonda, Gregory Peck, Steve McQueen and Barbra Streisand.

By June 1972, as the White House set out to undermine every American constitutional guarantee of the rights to privacy, free speech and equal justice, the proposal to break into the headquarters of the Democratic Party and tap their telephone lines seemed as trivial a breach of the law as a speeding ticket.

The Watergate break-in was so minor a part of the White House and CREEP election strategy that it is unlikely anyone bothered to tell President Nixon in advance about the project. But there is no doubt that within days of the burglars being caught, Richard Nixon joined the cover-up to try to prevent the world ever knowing how power-hungry and corrupt the White House had become.

At first, through the efforts of the White House, the cover-up looked like a solid wall of impenetrable perjury. But in the end, partly because of the mixed loyalties of James McCord, it was shown to be a flimsy tissue of lies.

Released on bail with the other accused men, McCord grew more and more restless as his trial approached. He was coming under pressure from White House officials to plead guilty to the charges — and to blame the shadowy influence of the Central Intelligence Agency for the burglary. McCord kept a meticulous diary of the White House approaches to him, including offers of money to buy his silence and support his family, and of clemency from the White House which would cancel out any jail sentence.

But the White House reckoned without the gritty integrity of District Court Chief Judge John Sirica, a tough no-nonsense Republican, a fellow member of Nixon's own political party.

Just two defendants, Liddy and McCord, pleaded not guilty to the charges, and even then they made only token defences. Judge Sirica was not content merely to accept the sullen consent of men who had agreed to plead guilty or who made only feeble protests of innocence. He postponed sentencing for two months, leaving the Watergate burglars in no doubt that he was giving them one more chance to consider telling the truth or face harsh jail terms.

One month later, unease among the members of the US Senate, both Republicans and Democrats, had reached the stage where they voted to conduct their own investigation into the Watergate scandal. That was enough for James McCord. When he appeared again before Judge Sirica, he revealed that senior White House officials had been involved in the break-in and the cover-up.

Now the power of the American judicial system was turned against the men who had tried to pervert it.

As the hearings began the staff of the White House and CREEP, who had plotted the massive conspiracy and tried to cover it up, were falling out among themselves. One by one they resigned their posts and began to face a series of trials before federal courts.

Only one man, Richard Nixon, held out against the barrage of public and judicial demands for the full truth to be revealed.

Claiming presidential privilege, Nixon refused to hand over any notes of conversations in the White House during the period immediately after the Watergate burglary, when, his aides were now admitting, it had been agreed to try to buy the silence of the burglars and to block any further investigations.

In June 1973, just 12 months after the Watergate break-in, the Senate Committee called White House legal counsel John Dean in front of the television cameras at their hearings.

And slowly fragments of the truth began to emerge.

In calm, unemotional terms Dean told of conversations with the

President when they had discussed raising $1 million for the Watergate burglars. Dean told the committee, apologetically: 'The Watergate matter was an inevitable outcome of excessive concern over leaks, an insatiable appetite for political intelligence, all coupled with a do-it-yourself White House, regardless of the law.'

Dean's testimony was electrifying. But with other senior White House officials refuting his account of events, it seemed totally unsupported. Who was to corroborate his story?

The answer came a few weeks later, as the hearings dragged on apparently endlessly and hopelessly.

The committee was carrying out a routine interview with Alexander Butterfield, a member of the White House internal security staff, trying doggedly to piece together a diary of events after the Watergate break-in, of when the President had talked with John Dean, when he had talked with his chief of staff H. R. 'Bob' Haldeman, of what was discussed at these meetings, and which version they could believe of who said what and when.

Butterfield provided the answer in one stunning revelation. Every conversation in Richard Nixon's private Oval Office in the White House was infallibly taped by hidden recorders. Nixon had insisted himself on the system being installed long before his re-election so that he could have a record of all historic conversations for his memoirs.

Now there need be no doubt about the guilt or innocence of President Nixon. The tape recordings would prove, if his own version was to be believed, that he heard the news of the break-in with surprise and anger and that he ordered a full inquiry to bring all the culprits to justice.

But with Richard Nixon nothing was that straightforward.

The President refused to release the tapes.

There were very many sensitive items of international importance recorded on those miles and miles of indexed magnetic tape. Most of the conversations did not relate to Watergate. They must stay secret, the President protested.

For another four months, Nixon fought a losing legal battle to avoid handing over any of his tape recordings to the Senate investigators.

Grudgingly he began to part with some of them, mainly tapes which hardly had any bearing on the Watergate cover-up but which did provide a grotesque insight into the private personality of the President.

The Watergate investigators for the Senate and the courts listened to the tapes to screen out any irrelevant conversations which could have prejudiced national security. In many cases they were left with long speeches from the President which they had to censor themselves — on the grounds of public decency.

Time and time again the phrase '*Expletive Deleted*' had to be inserted into the text to cover up the bouts of gross obscenity as the President of the United States discussed his own staff behind their backs or made his views known on the personalities of political leaders at home and abroad.

It was not the language of diplomacy and learned political discussion which came across on the tapes. It was the wild cursing and profane banter of a group of men who might have been drinking in a sleazy bar instead of discussing affairs of state in the hallowed chamber of the Oval Office of the White House. Whatever the content of the conversations, many Americans were shocked and disgusted by the tawdriness of its vocabulary.

But still the President held back from releasing the most vital tapes, especially that of his meeting with chief of staff Bob Haldeman on 23 June 1972.

It took a full year of delaying tactics by Nixon before the issue was presented to the Supreme Court, the highest judicial authority in the land. As the court voted unanimously to force him to hand over the tapes, the Congress of the United States also voted to hand down articles of impeachment against the President.

In spite of his exalted position and his claim of presidential privilege, Richard Nixon was facing the prospect of a trial for gross, criminal abuse of his high office.

The tape recording of the Oval Office meeting of 23 June was the vital piece of evidence which might prove his guilt or innocence. It had been his first meeting with Haldeman after the Watergate burglary. Had Nixon demanded to know the truth about the break-in or had he immediately conspired with Haldeman to hide the truth?

On 5 August 1974 President Nixon made the transcript of that tape public. The record of the conversation with Bob Haldeman was no more than a high-pitched humming noise.

The crucial conversation lasting eighteen and a half minutes had been wiped clean from the tape. It had happened by chance, Nixon explained, when his private secretary accidentally hit the 'erase' button on the tape machine as she prepared the transcript. No record of that conversation now existed.

It was the final blow to his credibility.

Three days later he announced his resignation.

His Vice-President Gerald Ford was sworn in to take his place. And one of Gerald Ford's first acts as President was to give a full and unconditional pardon to Richard Nixon, making him totally immune for all time from any prosecutions in the Watergate Affair.

The man who had helped to shape the destiny of the United States slunk off from the White House, embittered and disgraced. The most powerful man in the world had been brought down by an alert night watchman's discovery of a suspicious piece of sticky tape.

Richard Nixon, after his resignation as US President

Acknowledgements

The publishers would like to thank the following for their kind permission to reproduce the pictures used in this book:
Topham Picture Library 24, 27, 41, 42, 48, 51, 56, 59, 66, 73, 83, 89, 93, 119, 122, 131, 132, 147, 148, 154; Keystone Press Agency Ltd 13, 16, 31, 37, 55, 69, 99, 109, 159; Fox Photos Ltd 21, 46, 61